The Saga of Seaman

The Story of the Dog Who Went With Lewis & Clark

Also by Everett C. Albers

Seaman the Dog
Color/Activity Books
for Children

*Lewis and Clark Meet the American Indians, As told by
Seaman the Dog*, illustrated by Kimberly Eslinger
IBSN: 0-9674002-0-1

*Lewis and Clark Animal ABC Book As told by
Seaman the Dog*, illustrated by Kimberly Eslinger
ISBN: 0-9674002-3-6

The Saga of Seaman

The Story of the Dog
Who Went With
Lewis & Clark

Seaman's Tale in Verse
by Everett C. Albers

with an introduction
by James J. Holmberg

Northern Lights, ND Press
Bismarck, North Dakota
2002

Published in 2002 by Northern Lights, ND Press

1001 Arthur Drive
Bismarck, North Dakota
58501-2444
northernlightspress.com
editor@northernlightspress.com

Printed in Canada

10 9 8 7 6 5 4 3 2 1

First Printing

International Standard Book Number: 0-9717181-0-5
　　　The Saga of Seaman:
　　　The Story of the Dog Who Went with Lewis & Clark
　　　Seaman's Tale in Verse by Everett C. Albers
　　　with an introduction by James J. Holmberg

Library of Congress Control Number: 2002100304

The paper in this book meets the requirements of ANSI/NISO Z39.48-1992 (Permanence of Paper).

∞

On the web at seamanthedog.com

Excerpt from THE CAPTAIN'S DOG, copyright © 1999 by Roland Smith, reprinted by permission of Harcourt, Inc.

Dedication

To my children
Albert Otto and Gretchen Alene
and the love of my life,
my wife Leslie —

Contents . . .

Illustrations . . .

Cover Art:

The image of Seaman on the front and on the facing page — looking particularly sagacious and a bit sad — was adapted from an undated, unattributed lined drawing purchased on an Internet auction. The image of the Scriver bronze of **Meriwether Lewis and 'Our Dog' "Scannon"** (54) is courtesy of the Lewis and Clark Trail Heritage Foundation, Inc.

Other Illustrations:

Line drawings of Seaman, pages 1, 13,14, 34, and 35 by Lili Stewart of Dickinson, North Dakota.

Images of Lewis (2), Clark (3), Shawnee Warrior (4), geese (12), buffalo calf (13), pronghorn antelope (15), beaver (16), buffalo (17), grizzly (18), wounded deer (19), Corps meets the Shoshone (20), the Corps in the Bitterroots (21), "Lewis and Clark on the Columbia" by Frederic Remington (22), Fort Clatsop (22), moose (24), Drawing of Mandan villages (28), Return to St. Louis (29), Mémin painting of Lewis (32), and Byron and Lewis (37) are from ArtToday, ©2000-2002-www.arttoday.com.

The keelboat on page 5 is courtesy of Lewis and Clark State Park, Onawa, Iowa.

The reproductions of the woodcuts on pages 6, 7, 25, and 26 are from one of the Mathew Carey editions of the journals of Patrick Gass, first published with illustrations in 1810.

The adaptations of paintings by R.W. Smith, "Lewis & Clark arriving at a Mandan village," SHSND 11549 (page 7) and Vernon Erickson, "Lewis & Clark meeting Sacagawea," SHSND 1985.22 (page 11) are from the collections of the State Historical Society of North Dakota.

The adaptations of paintings by Karl Bodmer (8, 27,30) are courtesy of The North Dakota Lewis & Clark Bicentennial Foundation.

Reproductions of references to the original journals (40, 41) are courtesy of the Lewis and Clark Trail Heritage Foundation, Inc.

The thumbnail reproductions of book covers cited in the "Author's Note" are included as a courtesy to the publishers and authors under the fair-use provision of the Copyright Act of 1976, with the permission of the publishers whenever possible (42, 44, 48, 58, 59)

The map on page 36 was created by the author.

All other images are from the author's collection, either gleaned from public domain sources or photographed by the author, including the images of the statues and monuments on page 9, 10, 11, 30, 31, 33, and 39.

Acknowledgements . . .

James J. Holmberg of the Filson Historical Society tracked down the proof that Seaman made it back home. He is singularly responsible for discovering Rev. Timothy Alden's reference to Seaman's collar and the answer to "What happened to Captain Lewis's dog?" in a publication in 1814, no more than five years after Lewis's death. Holmberg has edited a collection of letters from William Clark to his older brother, Jonathan, that will be published in the Yale Western Americana Series in May 2002 — *Dear Brother: Letters of William Clark to Jonathan Clark*. I am most grateful to Jim for his many suggestions, his gracious introduction, and for our growing friendship.

The entries from the journals of the members of the Corps of Discovery included in this book are from the University of Nebraska Press edition of the *Journals of the Lewis and Clark Expedition* edited by **Gary Moulton** and are used by permission of the University of Nebraska Press. Nearly every day over the last several years, I have taken down one of Gary's volumes to check the journals and whispered a thanks for his gift to all those who would read the story of America's greatest adventure.

I am, at best, an amateur historian, a rather indiscriminate (I prefer eclectic) reader, and a writer who needs much more editing than I can give myself. The two scholars of the Lewis & Clark Expedition I most admire, **James P. Ronda** and **Clay S. Jenkinson**, offered inspiration and encouragement. In nearly every page of such books as *Lewis and Clark among the Indians* and the exquisite *Finding the West: Explorations with Lewis and Clark*, Jim Ronda astonishes me with his insights and fresh perspectives. Clay Jenkinson in his book *The Character of Meriwether Lewis: "Completely Metamorphosed" in the American West* gives me what only the best humanities texts can: a challenging new way of thinking about the oldest of human questions. Recently, I heard my two friends, Jim and Clay, comment upon a couple of pages of journal entries for an hour in a public forum. The audience was absolutely delighted, enlightened, and mightily challenged. It is their public humanities work that inspired me to attempt *The Saga of Seaman*.

The Lewis and Clark Trail Heritage Foundation, Inc. give its kind permission to quote from its publication *We Proceeded On* (*WPO*), especially the *WPO Publication No. 10* (September 1990), "The Lewis and Clark Expedition's Newfoundland Dog," and, of course, James J. Holmberg's article "Seaman's Fate?" which appeared in *WPO* in February 2000.

The excerpts from the books about Seaman for young readers are printed with permission of the publishers credited in the "Author's Note."

Special thanks to the members and staff of the **North Dakota Humanities Council**, where I've worked for the past twenty-eight years. Here at this desk at the Council's office in the evenings and on weekends, I've been able to use what I've learned at this job to do projects like this one.

My daughter, **Gretchen Alene Albers**, read my manuscript carefully, found dozens of errors, offered scores of useful suggestions, and offered the kind of criticism I most needed, when I most needed it. I would never have attempted to tell this story in verse were it not for the way in which Gretchen and her brother, **Albert Otto Hermanson-Albers**, encouraged me with their enthusiastic response to my literary efforts for them when they were children.

My greatest debt, and my deepest gratitude, go to my wife of more than a quarter century, **Leslie Rae Albers**, whose unflagging support, incredible patience, and love so great that she never complains when I embark on a project like this, even when I start ordering up out-of-print books, mumble variations on verses while we travel in the car, and leave household chores unattended for weeks when I become preoccupied with such as *The Saga of Seaman*.

Introduction . . .

"His faithful dog shall bear him company."
Alexander Pope, *An Essay on Man*, Epistle I

The epic journey of the Corps of Discovery — best known as the Lewis and Clark Expedition — is one of the great chapters in American history. It is the story of bravery, hardship, friendship, danger, and cooperation between different cultures and peoples. Various names associated with this adventure have become famous: the captains, Meriwether Lewis and William Clark; the young Shoshone woman, Sacagawea, and her baby boy Pomp; Clark's African American slave York, the first black American to cross the United States from coast to coast. There are others whose names have entered the annals of expedition history that are widely recognized; men such as John Colter, George Drouillard, Sergeant Charles Floyd, and Sergeant John Ordway. Others have been forgotten, often unfamiliar to even Lewis and Clark enthusiasts.

There is another expedition member, however, that intrigues and delights not only the expedition enthusiast but the casual inquisitor. This is the only non-human member of the Corps of Discovery; an expedition veteran also deserving of the praise and recognition received by his human companions. That member is Seaman, Captain Lewis's faithful Newfoundland dog.

First appearing in expedition history in Lewis's journal entry for September 11, 1803, he appears occasionally for the next three years, making his final appearance on July 15, 1806. From his talent for catching swimming squirrels to his howling in pain at suffering the torment of hoards of mosquitoes, and many an adventure and misadventure in between, the loyal and stalwart companion of his master intrigues almost everyone and inspires one of the great canine stories in history. Evidence indicates that he played the role of "man's best friend" to the very end, choosing death on his master's grave to life without him.

Our fascination with Seaman is evident by his frequent appearance in Lewis and Clark-related books, articles, and art. With the approach of the Lewis and Clark bicentennial, Seaman's appearance in these various mediums have increased and undoubtedly will continue to do so. In Everett C. Albers' *The Saga of Seaman: The Story of the Dog Who Went with Lewis & Clark*, Seaman's story is told through verse from the perspective of the "greatest traveller" of his species himself. From Meriwether Lewis becoming his master while preparing for the expedition to Lewis's sad fate at Grinder's Stand on the Natchez Trace in October 1809, Seaman relates not only his story, but the story of the greatest exploring venture in the history of the United States.

Complementing the verse throughout its length are illustrations and sidebars. The illustrations are drawn from a wide range of sources and the sidebars provide commentary on expedition history and members and quote journal entries regarding Seaman.

To this Everett Albers adds an informative and thoughtful "Author's Note" that serves as an excellent conclusion to the *Saga of Seaman*. From comments on the Newfoundland breed by Lord Byron to the discovery of Seaman's correct name and his appearance in current books and articles, Everett Albers surveys those sources, comparing, contrasting, analyzing, and drawing conclusions. The sources cited span the years 1803 to 2000 and offer a thorough review of Seaman literature. As in the verse portion of the book, sidebars and selected illustrations again add to and complement this section.

Many a famous writer has penned and many a famous line has been written on the attributes and character of "man's best friend." In 1844 English poetess Elizabeth Barrett Browning wrote about her friend in "To Flush, My Dog,"

> "Therefore to this dog will I,
> Tenderly not scornfully,
> Render praise and favor."

May we, as Everett Albers and others have done, render the same to Seaman — one of the most well-traveled, heroic, loyal, and famous dogs in history.

James J. Holmberg
Louisville, Kentucky
December 28, 2001

Preface...

Seaman, the dog who went with the Corps of Discovery, becomes more famous every year as the nation approaches the 200th anniversary of the Lewis and Clark Expedition. For most of those 200 years, few people knew his name or what happened to him after the last reference to him on July 15, 1806, when his friend Meriwether Lewis noted that "my dog howls with the torture he experiences from them [mosquitoes]. At the turn of the twenty-first century, there were two new novels for young readers about Seaman (Gail Langer Karwoski's *Seaman the Dog Who Explored the West with Lewis & Clark* and Roland Smith's *The Captain's Dog: My Journey with the Lewis and Clark Tribe*). My own 1999-2000 efforts for children include *Lewis and Clark Meet the American Indians as told by Seaman the Dog* and *Lewis and Clark Animal ABC Book as told by Seaman the Dog*, both color-activity books. There is renewed interest in Adrien Stoutenburg and Laura Nelson Baker's 1959 *Scannon: Dog with Lewis and Clark*. Scheduled for publication in 2002 is a children's book by Laurie Myers entitled *Seaman's Tale*.

We know his name, thanks to Donald Jackson. And we have a good idea of what happened to him and further proof that his name was indeed Seaman, thanks to Jim Holmberg. But there's a great deal we do not know with any certainty, for there are only about thirty references involving Seaman in twenty-six discrete incidents in all of the extant journals. His name is recorded in only a handful, including the naming of a creek for him on July 5, 1806. About one-half of all of the journal entries involve Seaman hunting. Few references offer the kind of detail that makes for novels and epic poetry: Lewis refusing to sell the dog he paid $20.00 for to Shawnee on November 16, 1803; Seaman staying out all night and worrying Lewis on April 25, 1805; Seaman nearly dying from a beaver bite on May 19, 1805; Seaman saving the sleeping Corps members from a stampeding buffalo on May 29, 1805; and Lewis prepared to kill the thieves who steal his dog on April 11, 1806. The following seventy-five verses are based on what the Corps of Discovery members wrote and the most recent scholarship. Of course, I conjecture. Here's what I conclude:

1. Meriwether Lewis and Seaman bonded from the moment they found each other and were inseparable from the time they met in 1803 until they died in the same place in 1809.

2. Captain Meriwether Lewis was essentially a loner who had great difficulty relating to other humans — including even Clark at times — on an emotional level. In many ways, Lewis was not an easy man to like or to love. At many times during the journey and in the three years following the return of the Expedition, Seaman was the *only* living creature who gave Lewis unconditional love.

3. Lewis returned Seaman's loyalty and love in a way that he was incapable of bonding with humans, with the possible exception of his concern at times for Clark — for he knew that the success of the Expedition depended upon the general well-being of his co-commander. When he does write about his dog, it is with great pride and genuine affection — from being "fearfull we had lost him altogether" when Seaman stayed out all night in April 1805 to his careful medical attention and fear that the beaver bite in May 1805 "will yet prove fatal to him." When the Watlalas steal Seaman in April 1806, Lewis is ready to kill to get him back.

4. Seaman and Lewis had the kind of relationship that Lord Byron had with his Newfoundland, Boatswain, and there ought to be a monument next to the one marking Lewis's grave outside of Hohenwald, Tennessee, that echoes the final line in Byron's tribute to his friend — "I never knew but one, — and here he lies." Perhaps an inscription on a statue like Robert Scriver's marvelous bronze,

> Remember me as the truest friend
> Of Meriwether Lewis, there at the end
> With the one I loved, as he loved me.

If ever a dog deserved greater recognition, it is Seaman.

Everett C. Albers
Bismarck, North Dakota
January 1, 2002

Come closer now ...

Come closer now,
  And I will tell you how
I went with Lewis and Clark,
  About where we went
  And about how I sent
Bears running with my bark.

I will tell to you
  My story true
About how we went so far
  Away from home,
  To where buffalo roam,
Beneath the Northern Star.

Seaman, my name,
  Traveling, my fame,
Going along with Lewis and Clark.
  A big Newfoundland,
  On a journey grand,
I went with Lewis and Clark.

Known for gentleness and sweetness, Newfoundland dogs stand over two feet at the shoulders, weigh about 150 pounds, and live an average life of eight to ten years.

Seaman was young, but not a pup, when Captain Meriwether Lewis bought him for $20.00 in 1803.

Captain Lewis met me
  In Eighteen O Three,
In Philadelphia town we met.
  When we saw each other,
  We liked one another
From the very moment we met.

Meriwether Lewis
(1774-1809)

Historians are not sure about when Seaman met Lewis. We know it was sometime in 1803, possibly as early as May in Philadelphia where Lewis was purchasing supplies for the journey, possibly as late as August in Pittsburgh where Lewis waited for the keelboat to be completed.

"Seaman you'll be,"
  Said Meriwether to me
The day we met on
      the banks of a river.
"And you'll always be
  The best friend to me,
As you and I travel together."

After a long wait for the keelboat, Captain Lewis began the journey down the Ohio on August 31, 1803 with "a party of 11 hands."

Downriver we started,
  Pittsburgh we departed,
In August of Eighteen O Three,
  With a few men and a boat
  That barely could float
On river running ever so lowly.

−2

We saw hundreds of squirrels,
　Making whirls, twirls and swirls,
As they swam from
　　　one shore to the other.
　And I jumped in and caught them,
　To Lewis I brought them,
To the boat, one after another.

At the Falls of the Ohio,
　Great Falls of the Ohio,
Meriwether's friend
　　　William we met.
　Clark was his last name,
　And he soon became
A friend I would never forget.

William Clark
(1770-1838)

The first reference to Seaman in the journals of the Corps of Discovery is on September 11, 1803, when Lewis writes, ". . . observed a number of squirrels swiming the Ohio and universally passing from the W. to the East shore they appear to be making to the south . . . — I made my dog take as many each day as I had occasion for, they wer fat and I thought them when fryed a pleasant food— many of these squirrils were black, they swim very light on the water and make pretty good speed— my dog was of the newfoundland breed very active strong and docile, he would take the squirel in the water kill them and swiming bring them in his mouth to the boat. . . . "

Lewis wrote about Seaman's skill again four days later on September 15, 1803: " . . . saw and caught by means of my dog several squirrels, attempting to swim the river, . . ."

We met the Shawnee...

Shawnee Warrior
(From an engraving by
Tardieu L'aine, 1826)

When we met the Shawnee
Near the Mississippi,
They tried to buy me
for three beaverskins.
But Meriwether said, "No,
I will not let him go
For hundreds of beaverskins."

"My Seaman is brave
And he knows how to behave,"
Said Lewis to the one who would buy me.
"He's worth more than gold,
And he'll never be sold.
I'll never sell Seaman for money."

Wrote Meriwether Lewis on November 16, 1803 —
"Passed the Missippi this day and went down on the other side after landing
at the upper habitation on the oposite side. we found here som Shawnee
and Delewars incamped; one of the Shawnees a respectable looking Indian
offered me three beaverskins for my dog with which he appeared much
pleased. the dog was of the newfoundland breed one that I prised much for
his docility and qualifications
generally for my journey and of course there was no bargain,
I had given 20$ for this dogg myself—"

At Camp Wood with the men,
 Soldiers, riverboatmen,
We spent rainy months
    getting ready,
 Till May Eighteen O Four,
 When we left with our Corps
Of men who were
    rough but ready.

*Poling and oaring
the keelboat*

Wrote William
Clark on July 5,
1804, " . . . we
came to for
dinner at a
Beever house,
Cap Lewis's Dog
Seamon went in
& drove them
out."

Clark wrote on
August 25,
1804, " . . . we
assended a
riseing
ground . . . and
the *Mound*
which the
Indians Call
Mountain of
little people or
Spirits . . . at
two miles
further or Dog
was So Heeted
& fatigued we
was obliged
Send him back
to the Creek."

In July of that year
 I made it quite clear
That I was a swimmer and hunter.
 I drove out some beaver,
 From their houses some beaver,
Proving I was a good hunter.

In August Eighteen O Four
 I went along to explore
Mounds of earth Indian people
    thought holy.
 Tired and sick from the heat,
 I had to make a retreat
To a creek where I soaked ever so slowly.

Up the Missouri . . .

Up the Missouri we went,
  On a river not meant
To be sailed or oared in a keelboat.
  Men pulled more than they sailed,
  But their strength never failed,
As they made it
     upriver in the keelboat.

Each day my friends wrote
  And always made note
Of how far we traveled each day.
  We found birds and beasts,
  And at night we had feasts,
And even had some time to play.

Captains Lewis and Clark holding a council with a group of Indians the Corps met on its journey up the Missouri in 1804. The woodcut is one of six first published in the 1810 edition of *The Journals of Patrick Gass.*

To the villages ...

We proceeded on,
  Till we came upon
The towns of the village people
  Who lived in earthlodges,
  Warm, cozy earthlodges,
The Mandan and Hidatsa people.

The Corps of Discovery arrived at the Mandan/Hidatsa villages near the confluence of the Missouri and Knife rivers, about 40 miles north of present-day Bismarck, North Dakota, in October, 1804. Seaman and the Corps stayed with these people until April 1805.

The Corps of Discovery arrives at one of the Mandan villages (Adapted from a R.W. Smith painting, "Lewis & Clark arriving at a Mandan village" [State Historical Society of North Dakota 11549])

We built home of wood,
  In the neighborhood,
Of these most friendly,
      most helpful people.
  We traded for food,
  Wild game we pursued,
With the Mandan and Hidatsa people.

Building Fort Mandan (From the 1810 edition of The Journals of Patrick Gass)

Inside a Mandan Earthlodge (adapted from a Karl Bodmer painting)

Some men froze toes,
  There where the wind blows,
And it snows, and it blows,
    and it snows.
But earthlodges are warm,
Even in a big storm,
When it snows, and it blows,
    and it snows.

*Winter at the Mandan/Hidatsa Villages
(Adapted from a Karl Bodmer painting)*

Nicknamed "Pomp" by Captain Clark because he was a "dancing little boy," Jean Baptiste Charbonneau was born on February 11, 1805.

We made many new friends
  Where the great river bends,
And a new baby was born that winter.
  Pomp was the name,
  Of the baby who came
In February of that cold winter.

Leaving Fort Mandan ...

Pomp's mother, you know,
　Was Sacagawea, who also
Was the wife of Toussaint Charbonneau.
　All three joined our Corps
　When we set out once more
Toward the mountains covered with snow.

*Sacagawea
and Pomp
(Statue on
Capitol Grounds,
Bismarck, ND)*

My friend Meriwether
　Brought us together
To leave on the Seventh of April.
　"It's time that we go
　With canoe and pirogue —
Our mission we must now fulfill."

Our great keelboat
　Down the river did float
Back to the town of St. Louis.
　With some of the men,
　Soldiers, riverboatmen,
The keelboat went back to St. Louis.

The Corps of Thirty-four ...

Captains
Meriwether Lewis
William Clark
(Lieutenant in
formal rank)

Sergeants
Patrick Gass
John Ordway
Nathaniel Pryor

Privates
William Bratton
John Collins
John Colter
Pierre Cruzatte
Joseph Field
Reubin Field
Robert Frazer
George Gibson
Silas Goodrich
Hugh Hall
Thomas Proctor Howard
Francois LaBiche
Jean Baptiste LePage
Hugh McNeal
John Potts
George Shannon
John Shields
John B. Thompson
Peter M. Weiser
William Werner
Joseph Whitehouse
Alexander Hamilton Willard
Richard Windsor

Non-Military Members
Toussaint Charbonneau
Sacagawea
Jean Baptiste Charbonneau
George Drouillard
York
Seaman

We left our good friends,
   Where the great river bends,
Where the Missouri
      and Knife rivers meet.
Two pirogues, six canoes,
   And men for the crews
Made up our exploring fleet.

With Lewis and Clark
   Our Corps did embark
Upon our great
      westward journey.
   There were sergeants three
   And privates twenty-three,
And six others on
      this great journey.

*Captains Lewis &
Clark
(standing),
York and Seaman
(left)
(statue by
Robert Scriver,
at Great Falls,
Montana)*

Pomp and his mother,
  Charbonneau and two other
  Humans also went west to the sea.
There was my friend
    George Drouillard
  (Most often spelled "Drewyer"),
Clark's servant, York, and me.

We thirty-four
  Made up the Corps
That departed in Eighteen O Five.
  From the villages in April,
  On the Seventh of April,
We left in Eighteen O Five.

Sacajawea (statue by Pat Mathiesen, 1944, located in Bozeman, Montana)

Lewis and Clark party meet Sacagawea and Charbonneau at the Mandan villages (adapted from a Vernon Erickson painting, "Lewis & Clark meeting Sakakawea" [State Historical Society of North Dakota 1985.22])

Before our return,
We had to sojourn
Over mountains and great trackless land.
To the great western ocean
We set out in slow-motion,
To go where our captains had planned.

Seaman chased the largest of game for the Corps. Sergeant John Ordway wrote on July 14, 1804, ". . . passed a handsome Sand beach on the South Side, where we Saw three large Elk the first wild ones I ever Saw. Capt. Clark & drewyer Shot at them, but the distance was too long, they Ran or trotted in to the River and Seamon Swam across after them. . . ."

When our hunters shot beasts
For our nightly feasts,
And deer or geese
would be in the water,
I would swim into the river
And back to shore would deliver
Birds and beaver, even otter.

John Ordway wrote on Thursday, April 18, 1805, "The wind rose so high that we could not go with the cannoes without filling them with water. detained us about 3 hours. one man killed another goose Seamon b. [brought] out we then proceeded on."

Seaman & The Buffalo Calf ...

Meriwether and I
   Walked shores nearby
The muddy Missouri River.
   A young buffalo calf
   Made friend Lewis laugh
By following him along the river.

A Buffalo Calf

Said friend Meriwether,
   "He does not know whether,
Seaman is friendly
      or someone to fear.
   He wanted protection,
   And I had no objection
To the buffalo calf walking so near."

Wrote Captain Lewis on April 22, 1805, "walking on shore this evening I met with a buffaloe calf which attatched itself to me and continued to follow close at my heels untill I embarked and left it. it appeared allarmed at my dog which was probably the cause of it's so readily attatching itself to me."

Seaman stays out all night...

Wrote Captain Lewis on April 25, 1805, "The wind was more moderate this morning, tho' still hard; we set out at an early hour. the water friezed on the oars this morning as the men rowed. about 10 oclock A.M. the wind began to blow so violently that we were obliged to lye too. my dog had been absent during the last night, and I was fearfull we had lost him altogether, however, much to my satisfaction he joined us at 8 Oclock this morning."

Later that April,
　　on Twenty-five April,
When water froze hard as could be,
　　Friend Lewis did worry
　　That his friend furry,
Was lost, that he had lost me.

I was out all one night,
　　And gave him a fright,
Thinking I would never return.
　　Until morning at eight,
　　I made my friend wait,
Not knowing of his great concern.

Seaman hunts the antelope . . .

Twice I caught an antelope,
One was swimming, one did lope
Too slowly to get away from me.
I was big, but quite fast,
And so I often did outlast
Animals trying to escape from me.

The Pronghorn Antelope, often called "goats" by Corps of Discovery journalists

Wrote Captain Lewis on April 29, 1805, ". . . the Antelopes are yet meagre and the females are big with young; the wolves take them most generally in attempting to swim the river; in this manner my dog caught one drowned it and brought it on shore; they are but clumsey swimers, tho' on land when in good order, they are extremly fleet and dureable."

Lewis wrote on May 5, 1805, "The party killed two Elk and a Buffaloe today, and my dog caught a goat [antelope], which he overtook by superior fleetness, the goat it must be understood was with young and extreemly poor."

Clark's entry for May 5, 1805 concludes, "we Camped on the Stard Side, our men killed three Elk and a Buffalow to day, and our Dog Cought an antelope a fair race, this animal appeared verry pore & with young."

Seaman bit by a beaver …

Wrote Captain Lewis on Sunday, May 19, 1805, "Capt Clark walked on shore with two of the hunters and killed a brown bear; notwithstanding that it was shot through the heart it ran at it's usual pace near a quarter of mile before it fell. one of the party wounded a beaver, and my dog as usual swam in to catch it; the beaver bit him through the hind leg and cut the artery; it was with great difficulty that I could stop the blood; I fear it will yet prove fatal to him."

Then in month of May,
   On the very worst day
Of the entire journey I made,
   A wounded brown beaver
   Used his teeth as a cleaver,
And my life started to fade.

He bit my leg sorely,
   Made me feel so poorly,
That Meriwether
      was afraid I would die.
   I was terribly weak,
   And feeling most bleak,
But the beaver died, not I.

I lived to regret
   That I swam in to get
The beaver shot by
      one of the men.
   It only makes sense
   That it was self-defense –
He would probably bite me again.

Seaman saves the Corps . . .

I was not laid up long,
   Soon I was feeling strong
Enough to be on guard each
      night when we camped.
   On May Twenty-nine
   From the other shoreline
A buffalo swam, and
      toward us he tramped.

I met him head-on
   Barked him begone
From the men sleeping
      in tents on shore.
   I saved Lewis and Clark
   With my mighty bark.
That night, I saved the Corps.

Captain Lewis wrote about Seaman chasing another buffalo on June 19, 1805: "After dark my dog barked very much and seemed extreemly uneasy which was unusual with him. . . ." Lewis orders a sergeant and two men to have a look. The sergeant returned ". . . & reported that he believed the dog had been baying a buffaloe bull which had attempted to swim the river just above our camp but had been beten down by the stream landed a little below our camp on the same side & run off."

Wrote Captain Lewis on May 29, 1805, "Last night we were all allarmed by a large buffaloe Bull, which swam over from the opposite shore and coming along side of the white perogue, climbed over it to land, he then alarmed ran up the bank in full speed directly towards the fires, and was within 18 inches of the heads of some of the men who lay sleeping before the centinel could allarm him or make him change his course, still more alarmed, he now took his direction immediately towards our lodge, passing between 4 fires and within a few inches of the heads of one range of the men as they yet lay sleeping, when he came near the tent, my dog saved us by causing him to change his course a second time, which he did by turning a little to the right, and was quickly out of sight, leaving us by this time all in an uproar with our guns in or hands, enquiring of each other the case of the alarm, which after a few moments was explained by the centinel; we were happy to find no one hurt."

Seaman at the Great Falls...

Captain Lewis wrote on Thursday, June 27, 1805, "... a bear came within thirty yards of our camp last night and eat up about thirty weight of buffaloe suit [fat] which was hanging on a pole. my dog seems to be in a constant state of alarm with these bear and keeps barking all night."

On Twenty-seven June
I barked 'neath the moon
All night at bears stealing
   our stores
Of buffalo fat
Hanging out at
A place where white water roars.

There at the Great Falls,
  Through rain storms and squalls,
The men hauled canoes
   up those steep hills.
  Day-in and day-out
  We went roundabout
The Great Falls, up those high hills.

At last we arrived
  With spirits revived
Above the Great Falls of the river.
  In July Eighteen O Five,
  Happy to be alive,
We slowly went higher upriver.

Seaman & needle grass ...

Beyond the Great Falls,
　Those high waterfalls,
Drewyer wounded a deer when he shot it.
　It jumped into the river
　With a shake and a shiver.
I caught it – back to shore, I brought it.

Wounded Deer in River

Captain Lewis wrote on July 15, 1805: ". . . here Drewyer wouded a deer which ran into the river my dog pursued caught it drowned it and brought it to shore at our camp."

On Sunday, July 21, 1805, Lewis recorded Seaman's goose-hunting prowess: ". . . we daily see great numbers of gees with their young which are perfectly featured except the wings which are deficient in both young and old. my dog caught several today, as he frequently dose."

The pest of the plains,
　Needle grass caused us pains,
As we traveled on
　　toward mountains shining.
We could not bypass
　That sharp needle grass.
Those plants left me
　　howling and whining.

Wrote Lewis of the needle grass on July 26, 1805, ". . . these barbed seed penetrate our mockersons and leather legings and give us great pain untill they are removed. my poor dog suffers with them excessively, he is constantly binting and scratching himself as if in a rack of pain."

Seaman meets the Shoshone . . .

In August Eighteen O Five,
   The Corps did arrive
At the camps of the Shoshone people.
   Sacagawea met her brother,
   And they hugged one another,
When we met the Shoshone people.

Meriwether Lewis wrote on Saturday, August 17, 1805, ". . . every article about us appeared to excite astonishment in their [the Shoshone's] minds; the appearance of the men, their arms, the canoes, our manner of working them, the back [black] man york and the segacity of my dog were equally objects of admiration."

William Clark wrote on the same day, ". . . every thing appeared to astonish those people. the appearance of the men, their arms, the Canoes, the Clothing my black Servent & the Segassity of Capt Lewis's Dog."

Cameahwait found me wise,
   And he was most surprised
That my friend York was so big
   and so strong.
   Sacagawea's brother,
   Cameahwait, her brother,
Talked with Lewis and Clark
   all night long.

The Corps of Discovery meets the Shoshone

Over the Bitterroots . . .

Camp Fortunate was the place
  Where we met, face to face,
With Sacagawea's Shoshone people.
  They had horses, and a guide
  To show us up the mountainside,
Over Bitterroots to the Nez Percé people.

We will always remember
  When we were hungry in September
Of the year Eighteen Hundred and Five.
  When we reached the Nez Percé people,
  Twisted Hair's Nez Percé people,
We were fortunate to be alive.

*The Corps
of Discovery
descends
the
Bitterroot
Mountains*

To the Pacific Ocean ...

*Reconstructed
Fort Clatsop*

Then down the river westward,
With new canoes
we went on toward
The roaring Pacific Ocean.
There we spent a long winter,
Cold and wet rainy winter,
At Fort Clatsop, near the ocean.

There at the end of our trail
We saw a beached whale
Lying on the sandy seashore.
The Corps made salt from the sea,
Hunted food constantly,
And saw the great California condor.

*"Lewis and
Clark on
Columbia"
(adapted
from a
painting
by
Frederic
Remington)*

Seaman is stolen . . .

With the Chinook
    and the Clatsop
  At our home at Fort Clatsop
We lived till
    March Eighteen O Six.
Then we set out
    for the mountains,
Eastward toward
    shining mountains,
Up white-water
    rivers and creeks.

On Eleventh night of April
  I let out a great yowl
When three Chinooks
    stole me from camp.
Three soldiers
    came to get me,
And I was given
    back quickly
To Meriwether
    waiting at camp.

Meriwether Lewis wrote on Friday, April 11, 1806, ". . . three of this same tribe of villains the Wah-clel-lars, stole my dog this evening, and took him towards their village; I was shortly afterwards informed of this transaction by an indian who spoke the Clatsop language, and sent three men in pursuit of the theives with orders if they made the least resistence or difficulty in surrendering the dog to fire on them; they overtook these fellows or reather came within sight of them at the distance of about 20 miles; the indians discoverying the party in pursuit of them left the dog and fled."

William Clark writes on the same day, ". . . one other fellow attempted to Steal Capt. Lewis's dog, and had decoyed him nearly half a mile we were informed of it by a man who Spoke the Clatsop language and imediately Sent three men with their guns who over took the Indians, who on their approach ran off and lift the dog— we informed the nativ's by Signs that if the indians insulted our men or Stold our property we Should Certainly put them to death. . . ."

—23

Back to Traveler's Rest . . .

To Traveler's Rest we finally came
In July, with our horses lame,
Where we planned our journey home.
With friend Lewis, I went north —
Clark and others did set forth
South to where buffalo roam.

July the Fifth brought in sight
A creek friend Lewis
viewed with delight,
One he named
"Seaman's Creek" for me.
On Seventh day of July I chased
A moose so ugly-faced
I could not bear him being there
close to me.

Seaman continues to hunt for the Corps on the return journey. On May 8, 1806 William Clark writes, ". . . all of our hunters returned Drewyer & P. Crusat brought in a Deer each & Collins wounded one which our Dog Caught near our Camp."

Meriwether Lewis made a note on July 5, 1806: ". . . to the entrance of a large creek 20 yds. wide Called Seamans' Creek. . . ." The discovery of this note by historian Donald Jackson led to his conclusion that Lewis's dog was named "Seaman." Today, the stream named for Seaman is called Monture Creek. On July 7, 1806, Lewis notes, ". . . Reubin Fields wounded a moos deer this morning near our camp. my dog much worried."

Seaman battles the mosquitoes . . .

Eighteen O Six in July
  Mosquitoes made me cry,
And I howled both night and day.
  I was fast asleep on the night
  Blackfeet thought that it was right
To take our rifles and horses away.

Lewis's note on the mosquitoes torturing his dog is the last reference to Seaman in the journals of the members of the Corps of Discovery.

"An American having struck a Bear but not killed him, escapes into a Tree"
(From the 1810 edition of The Journals of Patrick Gass)

Lewis writes on Tuesday, July 15, 1806, ". . . a little before dark McNeal returned with his musquet broken off at the breech, and informed me that on his arrival at willow run he had approached a white bear within ten feet without discover him the bear being in the thick brush, the horse took the allarm and turning short threw him immediately under the bear; this animal raised himself on his hinder feet for battle, and gave him time to recover from his fall which he did in an instant and with his clubbed musquet he struck the bear over the head and cut him with the guard of the gun and borke off the breech, the bear stunned with the stroke fell to the ground and began to scratch his head with his feet; this gave McNeal time to climb a willow tree which was near at hand and thus fortunately made his escape. the bear waited at the foot of the tree untill late in the evening before he left him, when McNeal ventured down and caught his horse which had by this time strayed off to the distance of 2 ms. and returned to camp. these bear are a most tremenduous animal; it seems that the hand of providence has been most wonderfully in our favor with rispect to them, or some of us would long since have fallen a sacrifice to their farosity. there seems to be a sertain fatality attatched to the neighbourhood of these falls, for there is always a chapter of accedents prepared for us during our residence at them. the musquetoes continue to infest us in such manner that we can scarcely exist; for my own part I am confined by them to my bier at least ¾ths of my time. my dog even howls with the torture he experiences from them, they are almost insupportable, they are so numerous that we frequently get them in our thrats as we breath.—"

Fight with the Blackfeet ...

We had quite a fright
  Our only deadly fight
On our journey to ocean and back.
  Two young Blackfeet men lay dead,
  So Meriwether quickly led
Us away from the place of attack.

Captain
Lewis's party
encountered
the Blackfeet
on July
26-27, 1806.
The fight
resulted in
the death of
two young
men. Lewis
was
wounded in
a hunting
accident on
August 11,
1806.

"Captain Lewis shooting an Indian" (From the 1810 edition of The Journals of Patrick Gass)

Then friend Lewis was shot
  By Pierre Cruzatte
While they hunted elk
    on the bank of the river.
  Wounded in his butt,
  With an accidental bullet,
Meriwether lay in a canoe
    traveling downriver.

Reunion and return ...

At last we met Clark and his party —
  All were healthy, all were hearty —
And we quickly followed a plan
  To go on downriver,
  Two days down the river,
To villages of our friends the Mandan.

On Fourteenth of August,
  Hot summer day of August —
Eighteen O Six was the year —
  We returned to our friends,
  Where the great river bends,
After more than four months and a year.

A Mandan village on the Missouri (adapted from a Karl Bodmer painting)

Down river we raced...

We said farewell to Pomp,
  Sacagawea and Pomp,
And headed on back to St. Louis.
  Down the river we raced,
  Our path we retraced,
And we quickly came back to St. Louis.

The men of the Corps,
  Live evermore
In stories of journeys grand.
  John Colter returned
  To the West, he did turn
Before we left Mandan land.

Drawing of Mandan village

Sergeant Floyd had died
  And was buried beside
The Missouri River
      in Eighteen O Four.
  We passed by the site
  Where he died that night
In August Eighteen O Four.

To St. Louis and Washington ...

Some others went back
   And retraced the track
We made on our great journey west.
   But before they went back
   To follow that track,
They went to St. Louis to rest.

Return to St. Louis

At St. Louis we arrived,
   All but one had survived,
A journey of
      eight thousand miles.
   From St. Louis to ocean,
   The Pacific Ocean,
And back — eight thousand miles.

Then to Washington we went,
   Where we did present
Our stories to the president.
   Thomas Jefferson was pleased,
   And his mind was eased,
That we returned from where we were sent.

Sacagawea & Charbonneau ...

Sacagawea became ill
 At Fort Manuel
In Eighteen Hundred Twelve in December.
 Her spirit departed,
 This earth, she departed,
But her name and her life we remember.

Her husband lived on,
 His life stretched beyond,
The time he was forty or fifty.
 Touissant Charbonneau
 Continued to go
West until he was eighty.

"Sacajawea and Jean-Baptiste" by Alice Cooper, 1905, in Washington Park in Portland, Oregon

Charbonneau (pointing to visiting Prince Maximilian) was in his mid seventies when he was painted by Karl Bodmer near Fort Clark in the early 1830s

York & Pomp . . .

York became free
  Eventually,
No longer a slave owned by Clark.
  Jean Baptiste Charbonneau
  (The baby Pomp that you know)
Went to live with
  friend William Clark.

*York & Seaman,
part of
statue by
Robert Scriver at
Great Falls, Montana*

He went to school and returned
  To the West where he learned
The ways of the Indian people.
  He became a great guide
  Known far and wide
As an explorer who knew Indian people.

JEAN BAPTISTE CHARBONNEAU

Although not all historians agree, many believe that the son of Sacagawea and Toussaint Charbonneau is buried in Malheur County, Oregon. The marker reads, "This site marks the final resting place of the youngest member of the Lewis and Clark Expedition born to Sacajawea and Toussaint Charbonneau at Fort Mandan (North Dakota) on February 11, 1805. Baptiste and his mother symbolized the peaceful nature of the "Corps of Discovery". Educated by Captain William Clark at St. Louis, Baptiste at age 18, traveled to Europe where he spent six years, becoming fluent in English, German, French and Spanish. Returning to America in 1829, he ranged the Far West for nearly four decades, as mountain man, guide, interpreter, magistrate and forty niner. In 1866, he left the California gold fields for a new strike in Montana, contracted pneumonia enroute, reached "Innskip's ranche", here, and died on May 16, 1866.

Captain Lewis's last journey ...

"Captain Meriwether Lewis," by Charles B.J.F. Saint-Mémin

Friend Meriwether became
A man of great fame,
The Governor of the great West,
Louisiana Territory,
Bought in Eighteen O Three,
The new American West.

My friend became sad,
Meriwether was sad,
Unhappy with his job and life.
In Eighteen O Nine,
September Eighteen O Nine,
He made the last trip of his life.

Lewis set off from St. Louis on September 4, 1809. In a letter to his brother Jonathan, William Clark wrote that Lewis was on his way to Philadelphia and to Washington "to write our Book (but more perticularly to explain Some Matter between him and the Govt.). . ." At the end of his letter, Clark says, "I assure you that he had done nothing dishonourable, and all he has done will Come out to be much to his Credit as I am fully purswaded."

As he traveled down the Mississippi, Lewis took time to write his will. According to those with him, he tried to kill himself twice. On September 17, 1809, Lewis wrote a letter to President Madison from Fort Pickering (today's Memphis, Tennessee) where he was detained by the commander who kept a suicide watch over him for several days. In his letter, Lewis promised to clear up the problems. He said, "Provided my health permits no time shall be lost in reaching Washington."

Lewis left Fort Pickering on September 29. With him was his servant, Pernier; Major James Neely, U.S. agent to the Chickasaw nation; and Neely's servant. On October 10, Lewis went on ahead to Grinder's Inn with Pernier while Neely and his servant stayed behind to catch some stray horses. Lewis died at the Inn the following morning after shooting himself twice several hours earlier.

Meriwether Lewis dies ...

In Tennessee,
  On October Eleventh, we
Were out on the Natchez Trace.
  There Meriwether died,
  And that night I cried,
There in that lonely place.

A round granite pillar, a broken shaft, marks the grave of Meriwether Lewis.

Ornithologist Alexander Wilson (1776-1813), who painted birds brought by Lewis from the American West, traveled to Lewis's grave and wrote a poem for him that reads, in part,

"Poor reason perished in the storm
And desperation triumphed here!
. . . .
Pale Pity consecrate the spot
Where poor lost Lewis now lies low.
. . . .
Affection's steps shall linger here,
To breathe her sorrow o'er the dead."

The marker on the monument on Lewis's grave in Meriwether Lewis Park just off the Natchez Trace Parkway, near Hohenwald, Tennessee, reads
"Meriwether Lewis
1774-1809.
Beneath this monument erected under Legislative Act by the State of Tennessee, A.D., 1848, reposes the dust of Meriwether Lewis, a Captain in the United States Army, Private Secretary to President Jefferson, Senior Commander of the Lewis and Clark Expedition, and Governor of the Territory of Louisiana.

In the Grinder House, the ruins of which are still discernible, 230 yards South of this spot, his life of romantic endeavor and lasting achievement came tragically and mysteriously to its close on the night of October 11, 1809.

The report of the Committee appointed to carry out the provisions of the Monument Act, contains these significant statements: "Great care was taken to identify the grave, George Nixon, Esq., an old surveyor, had become very early acquainted with the locality. He pointed out the place; but to make assurance doubly sure the grave was re-opened and the upper portion of the skeleton examined and such evidence found as to leave no doubt of the place of internment."

Seaman grieves ...

I lay down on the ground,
  Above the best friend ever found,
Near the road called the Natchez Trace.
  There I cried, there I sighed,
  There I pined till I died,
Above Meriwether at his resting place.

    There they buried me as well,
      There where I said my sad farewell
    To the best of friends, Meriwether.
      My collar found way
      To a museum where it lay
    Until a fire burned my collar of leather.

My name is Seaman ...

Inscribed on my collar,
  Words by some scholar,
Remain for you to read and pass on to all:
"The greatest traveller of my species.
My name is SEAMAN,
      the dog of captain Meriwether Lewis,
Whom I accompanied to
  the Pacifick ocean through
The continent of North America."

  I live on whene'er my story's told
    Of how I went with explorers bold
  From Pittsburgh town to Pacific sea.
    Remember me as the truest friend
    Of Meriwether Lewis, there at the end
  With the one I loved, as he loved me.

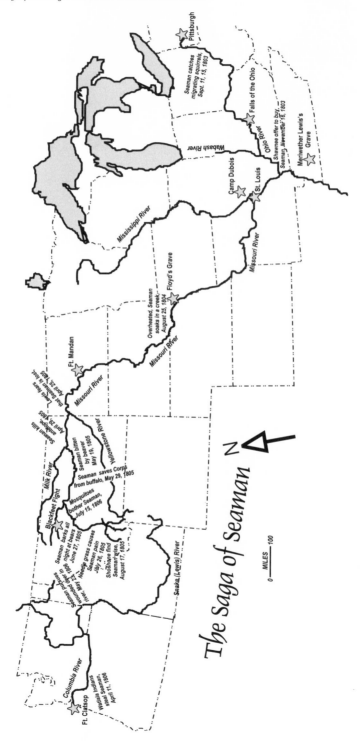

The Saga of Seaman

N

Seaman catches migrating squirrels, Sept. 11, 1803

Pittsburgh

Falls of the Ohio

Ohio River

Shawnee offer to buy Seaman, November 16, 1803

Meriwether Lewis's Grave

Wabash River

Camp Dubois

St. Louis

Missouri River

Overheated, Seaman soaks in a creek, August 25, 1804

Floyd's Grave

Mississippi River

Missouri River

Ft. Mandan

Lewis fears that Seaman is lost, April 25, 1805

Seaman kills antelope, April 29, 1805

Missouri River

Seaman bitten by beaver May 19, 1805

Milk River

Yellowstone River

Seaman saves Corps from buffalo, May 29, 1805

Mosquitoes bother Seaman, July 15, 1806

Blackfeet Fight

Seaman barks all night at bears June 27, 1805

Seaman shot clear through shoulder in wounds May, river, May 23, 1805

Needle grass causes Seaman pain July 26, 1805

Shoshone find Seaman wise, August 17, 1805

Snake (Lewis) River

MILES
0   100

Columbia River

Ft. Clatsop

Wallula Indians steal Seaman, April 11, 1806

Author's Note ...

IN NOVEMBER 1808, Governor Meriwether Lewis was busy in St. Louis in Louisiana Territory finding recruits for a likely war with Great Britain and doing his best to find a way to get the Mandan Chief Sheheke back to his village on the upper Missouri. In England, poet George Gordon, Lord Byron, was grieving the loss of his best friend, a Newfoundland dog named Boatswain. Governor Lewis's dog, Seaman, was still by his side. The Newfoundland he most often simply called, "my dog," had been his constant companion since the two met sometime in 1803, the year Byron's dog Boatswain was born.

Lord Byron (left) and Meriwether Lewis (right) shared more than chronic indebtedness and love for a Newfoundland dog. Remarkably similar in appearance, both lost their fathers at an early age (Byron was three, Lewis, five), both suffered from malaria attacks, and both died in their mid-thirties.

Like Byron, Lewis loved his loyal Newfoundland, who, after the return of the Corps of Discovery, wore a new collar inscribed with praise that began, "The greatest traveller of my species." After the successful return of the Corps of Discovery to St. Louis in 1806, Lewis went home to Virginia and on to Washington to report to President Jefferson. He then traveled to Philadelphia and back to Virginia once more, where he sought a wife in Albermarle County and in Fincastle, home of William Clark's fiancé. He traveled through Kentucky, including a stop at Louisville, and arrived in St. Louis early in March 1808 to assume his duties as governor. Seaman was with him.

Lewis's best human friend, William Clark, came to St. Louis with his new bride in the summer of 1808. Financially troubled, Lewis borrowed money from Clark regularly, including $49.50 on October 28, 1808 for two barrels of whiskey. Lewis was drinking heavily, and he took opium for his malaria, as many as three grams a night and two more in the morning. He had done nothing with the journals since his return from the Pacific Ocean. Unhappy and chronically depressed, unlucky in love and melancholic, Lewis was on a path to personal disaster. There was little comfort in most of his human relationships. But he could always count on his dog Seaman.

Lewis begins his thirty-first birthday meditation, "This day I completed my thirty first year, and conceived that I had in all human probability now existed about half the period which I am to remain in this Sublunary world. I reflected that I had as yet done but little, very little indeed, to further the hapiness of the human race, or to advance the information of the succeeding generation. I viewed with regret the many hours I have spent in indolence, and now soarly feel the want of that information which those hours would have given me had they been judiciously expended. but since they are past and cannot be recalled, I dash from me the gloomy thought and resolved . . ."

Just three years earlier, at the Great Divide among Sacagawea's Shoshone people, Lewis had vowed in his journal on his thirty-first birthday on August 18, 1805 to be

". . . resolved in future, to redouble my exertions and at least indeavor to promote those two primary objects of human existence, by giving them the aid of that portion of talents which nature and fortune have bestoed on me; or in future, to live for *mankind*, as I have heretofore lived for *myself.*—"

By late 1808, Governor Lewis had, in fact, done great good for his country. He managed to avoid an Indian war, and he had built a few roads. For himself, his brother, and friends, he worked hard to establish the St. Louis Missouri Fur Company, a private concern designed to monopolize trade at the mouth of the Yellowstone River after the government financed their expedition to return Sheheke to his village at the confluence of the Missouri and Knife rivers. Lewis hoped to make money to clear his many debts.

In England in 1808, the twenty-year-old Lord Byron had his own troubles with money and sex. Well on his way to earning his reputation as a "lover, lunatic, and poet," deeply in debt, Byron came to the nearly uninhabitable Newstead Abbey — a 300-year-old manor he inherited from a great uncle. After graduating from Cambridge, Byron moved to the heavily-mortgaged estate with his faithful dog and a tame bear. He slept in the supposedly haunted chambers of the former prioress of what had been a monastery. Attended by maids hired for their comeliness rather than their housekeeping skills, Byron entertained Cambridge cronies with ghoulish dinners at which he served Burgundy from a human skull.

When his faithful companion died of rabies, Byron completed one of the few improvements to his estate, an elaborate monument in memory of his dog.

Late in November 1808, he buried his Newfoundland, Boatswain. On the side of a pedestal supporting an antique urn, he had inscribed

**NEAR THIS SPOT
ARE DEPOSITED THE REMAINS OF ONE
WHO POSSESSED BEAUTY WITHOUT VANITY
STRENGTH WITHOUT INSOLENCE
COURAGE WITHOUT FEROCITY
AND ALL THE VIRTUES OF MAN WITHOUT HIS VICES
THIS PRAISE WHICH WOULD BE
UNMEANING FLATTERY
IF INSCRIBED OVER HUMAN ASHES
IS BUT A JUST TRIBUTE TO THE MEMORY OF
BOATSWAIN, A DOG
WHO WAS BORN AT NEWFOUNDLAND, MAY 1803,
AND DIED AT NEWSTEAD ABBEY,
NOVEMBER 18, 1808.**

Lord Byron also wrote a poem, "Inscription on the Monument of a Newfoundland Dog":

Byron's monument to Boatswain on the grounds of Newstead Abbey

When some proud son of man returns to earth
Unknown to glory, but upheld by birth,
The sculptor'd art exhausts the art of woe,
And stoned urns record who rest below;
When all is done, upon the tomb is seen,
Not what he was, but what he should have been;
But the poor Dog, in life the firmest friend,
The first to welcome, foremost to defend;
Whose honest heart is still his master's own,
Who labours, fights, lives, breathes, for him alone
Unhonour'd falls, unnoticed all his worth,
Denied in Heaven the soul he held on earth;
While man, vain insect! hopes to be forgiven,
And claims himself a sole exclusive of Heaven!
Oh, man! thou feeble tenant of an hour,
Debas'd by slavery, or corrupt by power,
Who knows thee well, must quit thee with disgust,
Degraded mass of animated dust!
Thy love is lust, thy friendship is all a cheat,
Thy smiles hypocrisy, thy words deceit!
By nature vile, ennobled but by name,
Each kindred brute might bid thee blush for shame.
Ye! who perchance behold this simple Urn,
Pass on — it honors none you wish to mourn:
To mark a friend's remains these stones arise;
I never knew but one, — and here he lies.

Newstead Abbey, November 30, 1808

NO SUCH MONUMENT OR POEM CELEBRATES the loyalty and life of Seaman, the dog who went with Lewis and Clark. For about one hundred years after the Expedition returned, no published journal named Captain Lewis's dog, and few Americans knew about his collar with his name in the museum in Alexandria, Virginia. When Sergeant John Ordway's journal resurfaced in 1913 and was subsequently published in 1916,[†] historians learned that the dog had a name — but what was it? Ordway's handwriting was difficult to read. Editor Milo Milton Quaife decided it was "Scannon." The famous Newfoundland's real name was finally determined in 1985, when Professor Donald Jackson published his article "Call Him a Good Old Dog, But Don't Call Him Scannon."[‡]

Lord Byron's Boatswain and Meriwether Lewis's Seaman are two of the most famous Newfoundland dogs. Among others are Leif Erickson's Oolum, the Newfoundland who accompanied him to North America, and another Newfoundland named Boatswain who rescued Napoleon Bonaparte when he fell overboard on his voyage from Elba to France.

From 1916 to 1985, Lewis's dog was called Scannon because of the way Ordway spelled "Seaman." The "e" was confused for a "c," the "m" for "nn" and the "a" in "man" either phonetically written or mistakenly read as an "o." The singular reference to Lewis's Newfoundland by Lewis or Clark was hidden in William Clark's *Field Notes*[††], found in 1953 in an old desk in an attic in St. Paul, Minnesota. Edited by Ernest S. Osgood, the *Notes* were published in 1964. Clark wrote ". . . we came to for Dinner at a Beever house, Cap Lewis's Dog Seamon [a Clark phonetic rendition of Seaman] went in & drove them out," Osgood corrected the name to read "Scannon."

William Clark's reference to "Cap Lewis's Dog Seamon" on July 5, 1804.

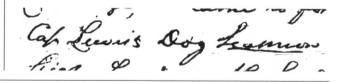

[†]Milo M. Quaife, ed, *The Journals of Captain Meriwether Lewis and Sergeant John Ordway: Kept on the Expedition of Western Exploration, 1803-1806* (Madison: State Historical Society of Wisconsin, 1916).

[‡]*We Proceeded On* 5 (July 1985), later included in Jackson's book, *Among the Sleeping Giants: Occasional Pieces on Lewis and Clark* (Urbana: University of Illinois Press, 1987) and one of two monographs in "The Lewis and Clark Expedition's Newfoundland Dog," *We Proceeded On*, WPO Publication No. 10 (September 1990).

[††]Ernest S. Osgood, ed. *The Field Notes of Captain William Clark, 1803-1805* (New Haven: Yale University Press, 1964).

Top — Ordway's handwritten entry in his journal for May 8, 1806 refers to "Capt. Lewises dog Seamon," which editor Quaife read as "Scannon."

Bottom — the earlier entry by Ordway to "Seamon," April 16, 1805, which Quaife read as "Scamon."

Lewis's dog continued to be called Scannon until Donald Jackson pondered the brief reference in the journal of Meriwether Lewis on July 5, 1806 to a "large creek 20 yds. wide Called Seamans' Creek," Clark's reference on the same day to "Seamons Creak," Clark's notation on a sketch map to "Seamons Creek," and Clark's entry of July 5, 1804. Jackson himself thought that the references might be a garbled version of "Scannon" until he examined the original manuscripts, including John Ordway's journal.[†]

Ordway sold his journal to Lewis and Clark.[‡] In 1810, Clark gave the journal to Nicholas Biddle, who arranged for editing and publishing of Lewis and Clark's journals, but not Ordway's.

[†]Donald Jackson concluded, "No person named Seaman is known to have been associated with the lives of either captain, and as a common term the word seems strangely nautical in view of its location. When it became necessary for Lewis and Clark to name a creek, river, or other geographical feature, they were predictably direct and simple in their choices. . . . They usually went straight to the heart of the matter and chose a sound, reasonable name for the simplest of reasons: to commemorate a member or sponsor of the expedition.

"It occurred to me that the name might be a garbled version of Scannon's Creek, in honor of the faithful dog. The dog had been with Lewis on that side trip, and no geographical feature had yet been named for him during the entire expedition. I consulted microcopies of the journals held by the American Philosophical Society, half suspecting I would find that Seaman's Creek was actually Scannon's Creek. What I learned instead was mildly startling. The stream was named Seaman's Creek because the dog's name was Seaman." — Donald Jackson, *Among the Sleeping Giants: Occasional Pieces on Lewis and Clark* (Urbana: University of Illinois Press, 1987).

[‡]Most scholars agreed that Lewis and Clark paid Ordway $300. Kerry Oman in her essay, "Serendipity," *We Proceeded On* (November 2001), found evidence that Ordway intended to publish his journal until Lewis persuaded him otherwise. Oman also found a reference in an 1904 publication stating that Ordway was paid ten dollars, not $300.

Biddle returned all of the original manuscripts to Clark — except for Ordway's and those kept by Lewis and later Clark of the journey from Pittsburgh to Camp Dubois, from August 31 to December 12, 1803. Biddle's grandsons discovered these journals in 1913, and they were edited by Quaife for publication by the State Historical Society of Wisconsin in 1916. With Ordway's journal and Clark's *Field Notes*, Captain Lewis's dog finally had a name.[†]

Cover of Scannon: Dog with Lewis and Clark *by Adrien Stoutenburg and Laura Nelson Baker, illustrated by Stephen Cook (New York: Charles Scribner's Sons, 1959).*

Roger Emerson and John Jacobson, "The Adventures of Lewis and Clark (Musical)," Hal Leonard.

There were hints in the Ordway manuscript that Lewis's dog was not named Scannon, the spelling adopted by Quaife. In their note to the 1959 *Scannon, Dog with Lewis and Clark,* authors Adrien Stoutenburg and Laura Nelson Baker wrote, "Ordway's handwriting was not always clear, so sometimes the dog's name appears to be 'Scammon' or 'Semon'."

Nonetheless, Seaman was "Scannon" for sixty years, and hundreds of Newfoundlands were named Scannon from 1916 to 1985. Lewis's dog "Scannon" is one of the stars of the musical meant to be performed by children; he sings "Life's 'Ruff!'" to a Charleston dance tune — a litany of the woes of one "who did the entire trip on four little paws, and not a hydrant in sight."

Few Newfoundland owners called their dogs "Brewster," the name given Lewis's dog by his eclectic biographer Charles Morrow Wilson in 1934.[‡] Apparently, Wilson did not read Quaife — or even know of the early journals of Lewis or Ordway's journal (the publication does not appear in his bibliography). "Brewster," writes Wilson, was "a foot-loose and homeless mongrel" found by Lewis "in the port

---

[†]Ernest Staples Osgood, "Our Dog Scannon — Partner in Discovery," first published in *Montana, The Magazine of History* 26 (July 1976), pp. 8-17 and Donald Jackson, "Call Him a Good Old Dog, But Don't Call Him Scannon" (see note, page 40) are collected in "The Lewis and Clark Expedition's Newfoundland Dog," *We Proceeded On*, WPO Publication No. 10 (September 1990). The publication is still available from WPO Publications, P.O. Box 3434, Great Falls, Montana 59403.

[‡]Charles Morrow Wilson, *Meriwether Lewis of Lewis and Clark* (New York: Thomas Y. Crowell Company, 1934).

of St. Louis." Wilson does not identify the dog as a Newfoundland, but does say that "He was powerful, fleet and good-natured, highly competent at trailing game, joining frolics, and woofing at passersby. Brewster was a promising addition [to the Corps of Discovery]."

During the winter among the Mandan and Hidatsa in 1804-1805, Wilson has Captain Lewis wandering the surrounding prairies with his gun and dog until it becomes so cold that

> Meriwether found himself robbed of all chances for solitary wanderings. Even when he put on all the clothes he had and a buffalo robe or two besides, he still couldn't be secure against frostbite; so he retreated to the headquarters tenanted by Clark and took Brewster as the third companion. The choice showed more sentiment than wisdom, for Brewster had become sorely infested with fleas, and spent most of the days and a good part of the nights at whining and scratching himself.

But once the Corps reaches the mouth of the Yellowstone on their outward journey to the Pacific, Lewis is again walking ashore,

> . . . Brewster trailing joyously at his heels or frolicking through the brambled forests pursuing unseen trails. Sometimes the black mongrel overdid it, for during this state of the journey the Virginian repeatedly lost his dog and worried greatly; but invariably day-break would find Brewster back at his master's side, ready for another day of exploration.

None of the Corps journalists mention Seaman at Fort Mandan.

There is, in fact, evidence in the journals that Seaman was lost — on one occasion, Lewis was indeed concerned about Seaman until he returned after being out all night on April 25, 1805.

Charles Morrow Wilson's biography of Lewis is rarely — if ever — acknowledged by professional historians — not even in a bibliography. For example, there is no reference to his book in Stephen E. Ambrose's *Undaunted Courage*. Richard Dillon's *Meriwether Lewis: A Biography* (New York: Coward-McCann, 1965) dismisses Wilson with a quote from Vardis Fisher's *Suicide or Murder? The Strange Death of Governor Meriwether Lewis* (Chicago: Swallow Press, 1962) — "a farrago of errors."

Wilson (1905-1977) of Arkansas and later Vermont was a freelance writer, part-time reporter for the *New York Times* and executive of the United Fruit Company at various times in his life. He wrote biographies of Rudolf Diesel (the inventor of the Diesel engine), Geronimo, and William Jennings Bryan. Other works include fiction and *The Magnificent Scufflers* (a history of wrestling), *The Dred Scott Decision*, and *The Story of the American Banana Trade*. His nonfiction articles include several versions of a controversial article about Arkansas governor Orval Faubus for *Reader's Digest*. Wilson's papers — nearly 40 linear feet — are in the Selected Manuscript Collections in the Special Collections Division of the University of Arkansas Library at Fayetteville.

Wilson also includes the incident involving Lewis's dog a year later on the return trip from the Pacific, when Indians steal "Brewster":

> Troubles, however, couldn't stay away. River Indians were skilful thieves. When night camps were made, blankets and trinkets disappeared in spite of tired watchmen and the uproarious vigilance of Brewster. Then one night by way of climax, the Indians stole the dog. Meriwether Lewis was more than warm . . .

Wilson quotes a long passage from Lewis's journal of April 11, 1805,[†] which details the capture and release of Seaman after Lewis sent three men after the thieves. Concludes Wilson,

> . . . it was the first time he [Lewis] had used the threat of death; but stealing a man's dog makes a difference.

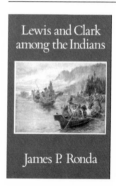

Lewis and Clark among the Indians

James P. Ronda

[†]In his masterful book *Lewis and Clark among the Indians* (Lincoln and London: University of Nebraska Press, 1984), historian James P. Ronda summarizes the events of April 11, 1805 with delightful understatement and powerful narrative skill:

"No sooner had the portage [around the Cascades] begun than the Watlalas commenced their delaying tactics. So many Indians crowed around the base camp that several extra men had to be assigned to guard duty. The harassment increased when one particularly bold Indian began throwing stones down on two men in the portage party. John Shields, who had taken some extra time at the head of the Cascades to buy a dog, suddenly found himself the object of the Watlalas' attention. When several Indians attempted to take his future meal and push him off the portage path, Shields drew his knife in readiness for something more than a polite scuffle. Seeing his determined resistence, the native highwaymen fled. Even Lewis did not escape his share of trouble. Three Watlalas slipped into his camp at dusk, and before he could stop them, they had absconded with the dog Scannon [Ronda wrote his book before his mentor Donald Jackson discovered Seaman's real name]. Gunplay was fortunately avoided as the Indians released the dog when they saw armed explorers in hot pursuit. Not even the reassurances of a Watlala chief that these were the unsanctioned exploits of "two very bad men" and "not the wish of the nation" could mollify the Americans. Lewis and Clark ordered the sentries to shoot any Indian who dared steal the expedition's property. The Watlalas may have seen this all as a baiting game, but an edgy Lewis did not share that view. "I am convinced," he wrote, betraying both worry and belligerence, "that no other consideration but our number at this moment protects us."

Wilson places Brewster with Lewis after his flight from the scene of the encounter with the Blackfeet that resulted in the death of two young Indian warriors, and the dog helps flush out the elk that Lewis and Pierre Cruzatte were hunting when Cruzatte accidentally shoots Lewis in his left thigh about an inch below his hip joint on August 11, 1806:

> Brewster barked frantically, and Meriwether Lewis stumbled to the ground with a flesh wound in his left thigh. The lead ball had cut deep, and the Virginian called to his companion:
>
> "Damn you, man you've shot me!"
>
> He heard no answer and, groaning, struggled to his feet and with the puzzled Brewster at his side, hobbled back toward the river, shouting to his follower that there were Indians about.
>
> . . . .
>
> Patrick Gass called the band together and made camp, and in company with Brewster kept watch over the wounded commander.

The final reference to Brewster in Wilson's biography of Lewis comes after the discharge of the Corps in St. Louis in October 1806:

> Disbanding his Corps was no easy duty. His men had become comrades and friends. Now that the journey was finished and the day for parting was at hand, most of the Corps chose discharge so that they might take advantage of the promised bounty of government lands. Only three, McNeal, Windsor, and Goodrich, reënlisted in the slumbering Army.
>
> Still accompanied by Brewster, Lewis spent a considerable part of this time in St. Louis at strolling through the forest lands that adjoined the sunwashed village.
>
> As a soldier, he had gained his mission. His Corps had been the first to cross the North American continent by land; an epoch-making feat, news of which would travel throughout the

In addition to calling Seaman "Brewster" and placing him at the scenes of the Blackfeet encounter and the hunting accident on the return journey (there are no references in any of the journals of the Corps of Discovery), Wilson mistakenly makes George Drouillard, not Cruzatte, the culprit who accidently shoots Lewis (as do Emerson and Jacobson, in "The Adventures of Lewis and Clark"). Wilson misspells his name, puts him in the army — "Private Druillard" (the interpreter and scout did not enlist), and makes him half-blind (that was Cruzatte, not Drouillard).

Wilson did do considerable research, for he correctly identifies three of the men who returned to the army after the return of the Expedition — although Richard Windsor probably settled in Missouri before rejoining. However, others also found their way back to army life, and several served in the War of 1812.

civilized world. He had kept on to the last mile of the way. He had gambled his life and his military career, and he had won.

The years had matched his cards. Now maturity and middle age were upon him, in his blood and spirit and muscle. He was sad, and he could not make due explanation of the sadness not even to himself.

William Clark, a happy warrior, was superbly contented with the village's rounds of revelry. Escorted by York, the Kentuckian made unending rounds of revelry and taverns and dinners and balls, radiating good cheer and gallant sentiments.

The Virginian stayed much to himself. The taverns seemed to have turned cheap tawdry. Frolics were empty and mocking. He had lost his appetite for merrymaking and he found little pleasure either in uniforms or in women, and that, for a soldier, is a sorry state of being. He continued to wear an outfit of buckskin.

William Clark protested at his undue moodiness. Meriwether Lewis made kindly answer. He didn't mind living particularly so long as he could walk alone. New work would bring him new happiness, and he would be finding new work.

Middle October saw the Corps discharged and all but the two officers and the Indians gone their way. The Mandans all being completely weary of St. Louis, were anxious to have none of the formal pow-wows with white men.

By now Meriwether Lewis had suffered another bereavement, which not even William Clark could solace. His dog, Brewster, was to go. The black mongrel, after six thousand miles of unwavering loyalty, turned feeble on his return to civilization. The dog was aging.

Lewis administered a mixture of vermifuge and calomel, and then when doctorings proved of no avail, he brought Brewster into his room and gave him a woolly buffalo robe to sleep on. Brewster looked upon his master in pathetic gratefulness, but spurned all offers of food. Next morning the Virginian woke to find his dog dead, head forward, between outstretched paws, as if in prayer. Meriwether Lewis was very sad indeed.

Lewis was indeed a loner, but he did not spurn a celebratory drink or new clothes. In fact, one day after the Expedition returned, Lewis and Clark visited a tailor.

If Seaman went from St. Louis to the Pacific and back, the journey was over eight thousand miles, not six thousand — not counting the journey from Pittsburgh to St. Louis in 1803.

Not even the faithful Seaman would have "looked upon his master in pathetic gratefulness" after being given a combination of a dewormer and purgative — it must have been the buffalo robe that made him thankful.

For two days Captain Lewis recruited his party for the return to Washington, the Mandans, William Clark and their generous host, Auguste Choteau. The Virginian decided to go by river board [boat] as far as Wheeling, thence by stage to Washington town. His return to Albemarle he postponed, for the east-bound river boats were slow and Lewis reckoned on going as early as possible to the Capital in hopes of gaining the most generous pay possible for his Corps.

On the seventeenth of October, the very day of the start, Thomas Jefferson was delivering a message to Congress, beseeching generous rewards for all the Corps of Western Discovery.

Wilson makes it difficult for historians to take him seriously: Lewis left for the East in October; he stopped at home in Virginia before going to Washington; and Pierre, not Auguste Choteau went east with Lewis. Jefferson did not even know that the Corps had returned until later in October 1806, and he did not appear before Congress but sent a written message to Congress on December 2, 1806.

As an historian of the Lewis and Clark Expedition and biographer of Meriwether Lewis, Charles Morrow Wilson was, at best, less than rigorous in his attention to details and factual information. But for all of his mistakes — more than enough to justify Vardis Fisher's dismissal of his work as a "farrago of errors," Wilson does remarkably well in his characterization of Meriwether Lewis as a loner who returned from the American West a changed man. Moreover, his view that Lewis did indeed commit suicide is generally accepted by historians at the beginning of the twenty-first century, including Stephen E. Ambrose, whose pithy conclusion in *Undaunted Courage** stands as the succinct judgement of those who have examined the evidence:

> There is a considerable literature on the possibility that Lewis did not commit suicide but was murdered. The first to put forth that claim in any detail was Vardis Fisher.[†] Dr. Chuinard has more recently made the same assumption.[‡] The literature is not convincing; the detailed refutation by Paul Russell Cutright is.[††]

---

*Stephen E. Ambrose, *Undaunted Courage: Meriwether Lewis, Thomas Jefferson, and the Opening of the American West* (New York: Simon & Schuster, 1996), page 477.

†Vardis Fisher, *Suicide or Murder? The Strange Death of Governor Meriwether Lewis* (Chicago: Swallow Press, 1962).

‡Eldon G. Chuinard, "How Did Meriwether Lewis Die? It Was Murder," *We Proceeded On* 18 (January and May 1992).

††Paul Russell Cutright, "Rest, Rest, Perturbed Spirit," *We Proceeded On* 12 (March 1986).

In his biography of Lewis, Richard Dillon waffles and finally begs:

> Meriwether Lewis has not been proven guilty of self-destruction at Grinder's Stand in the early hours of October 11, 1809. Therefore, let him be found NOT GUILTY of the charge—the crime of suicide.[†]

Cover of Jenkinson's essays about Meriwether Lewis. Says historian James P. Ronda of the book, "This is certainly the most thoughtful, judicious study of Lewis so far. What Clay Jenkinson has written offers a portrait of a fully human character, someone filled with conflicts, tensions, ambiguities, and real accomplishments. He has written a very important book, one that deserves a wide and enthusiastic audience."

In the most recent biography of Lewis,[‡] Clay S. Jenkinson names his final chapter "Suicide" and offers a compelling argument that Lewis killed himself based on both the historical record and a remarkable read of Lewis's character in a book of humanities essays that offer new lenses on the troubled soul of Lewis.

No one knows Lewis better than Jenkinson, who brings the best of humanities perspectives from Homer, Ovid, and Plutarch to Shakespeare and Jonathan Swift to his interpretation of Lewis's character.

Jenkinson, a humanities generalist, offers several reasons for Lewis's depression, including one identified by Wilson. Indeed, no small part of Lewis's sadness, the depression complicated by drugs and alcohol (the self-abuse is largely ignored by Wilson and Dillon) had something to do with watching the stream of traders ascending the Missouri and his disdain for those flocking into Louisiana Territory, those Wilson calls "Down-and-outers from the States, riffraff and jailbirds, thieves and murderers and pillagers. . . ."

Had he lived to read *The Character of Meriwether Lewis*, Wilson would have been delighted with Jenkinson's scholarship and insights — especially his comparison of Lewis

---

[†]Richard Dillon, *Meriwether Lewis: A Biography* (New York: Coward-McCann, 1965).

[‡]Clay S. Jenkinson, *The Character of Meriwether Lewis: "Completely Metamorphosed" in the American West* (Reno, Nevada: Marmarth Press, 2000).

and Neil E. (Buzz) Aldrin — and his question, "When you've been to the moon, what's left?"

Wilson portrays a man who loved but once — and Aaron Burr's daughter Theodosia Burr Alston was not available. "Merne" Lewis (a curious nickname adapted by novelist Anya Seton in her *My Theodosia*) has one good human friend ("Billy" Clark), a surrogate father he cannot please (Thomas Jefferson, who keeps asking for the journals), and his dog, Brewster (the only living creature he does not disappoint).

How Wilson came up with the name Brewster, we may never know. We may discover evidence eventually that Lewis did harbor great affection for Theodosia Burr Alston† — like the rumors that Sally Hemings was Jefferson's mistress and that he was the father of her children, Lewis's love of Theodosia has been around a long time.

---

†The undocumented death of Lewis's dog just after the end of the Expedition is a small matter compared to Wilson's insistence that Lewis's one true love was Theodosia Burr Alston, Vice-President Burr's daughter whom he met at a dinner hosted by President Jefferson while Lewis was serving as his personal secretary. According to Wilson, Lewis spent delightful days teaching her to ride and even wrote a riding manual for her that Wilson says turned up later in the private papers of Aaron Burr. Lewis was so smitten, suggests Wilson, that he accommodated her late-sleeping habits and gave her lessons in the afternoon. "That required that the Virginian return to work, and keep at his desk until far past midnight."

Theodosia was the "only great passion of Meriwether Lewis's life," says Wilson. "When Merne Lewis sought to give words to his sentiments, Theodosia was pleasantly frank. As a suitor the captain was definitely past season. She liked him well enough, believed him a sterling young man blessed with a brilliant future; but Theodosia had a reputation and a husband to keep. Therefore the captain could remain a friend of the family's."

"That ended it. The Captain knew too much of discipline and dignity to rebel. If Theodosia could find no place for him in the locked walls of her heart, then as an officer and a gentleman he would go his way. Theodosia, smiling much, had termed the affair romantic idiocy. Meriwether excessively heavy of heart, went back to work; but he went back with sure conviction that they would meet again. . . ."

Wilson brings Lewis and Theodosia Burr Alston (1783-1813) together again at Aaron Burr's trial in 1807 in Virginia (Lewis was, in fact, there). After a pleasant conversation and a quiet dinner, they part. "Meriwether Lewis had meant to her simply another casual affair; but Theodosia had been principal of the Virginian's one enduring love, a love which no casual passing of months and years could turn to dust. Theodosia didn't understand. She would never understand."

Theodosia says "Good-night, Governor—until we meet again." Meriwether touches her hand and says, "We will never meet again."

Wilson did not take the time to footnote his conclusions, and no small part of his 1934 book probably relies on cultural gossip, something akin to urban legends of our time. His characterization of Clark's slave as a buffoon — "black as a hat, well over six feet tall, bullet-headed, ivory-toothed, and as stong as a gorilla" — says much more about blatant racisim in America in the 1930s than it does about York.

Anya Seton, the historical novelist, claimed in her preface to *My Theodosia*, "three separate sources" for the "Meriwether Lewis romance."[†] She did not name the sources.

However, Richard Dillon, whose book about Lewis is generally accepted as *the* biography, eschews both footnotes and bibliography, ". . . not because the author did not ponder hundreds, literally, of books and manuscripts . . . but solely because he finds himself "unable to better the thirteen-page bio-bibliographical appendix to Donald Jackson's remarkable collection of *Letters of the Lewis and Clark Expedition, With Related Documents*."[‡]

[†]Anya Seton, *My Theodosia* (Boston: Houghton Mifflin Company, 1941).

Theodosia is also at the center of one of America's great ghost stories. Wife of the wealthy Governor Joseph Alston of South Carolina, she left her husband's plantation on New Year's Eve in 1812 to visit her famous father in New York. The ship on which she sailed, *The Patriot*, was never seen again after the British stopped it and allowed it to pass off Cape Hatteras early in January 1813. By some accounts, pirates plundered the ship and killed all aboard. But legend has it that an old dying woman in 1869 identified herself as Theodosia, who had become a poor fisherman's wife after finding her way ashore in 1813. When the old woman offered to pay an attending physician with any item in her house, the doctor chose a portrait of a beautiful woman. The old woman said, "It's mine! You can't have it. I am taking this picture of his darling Theodosia to my father in New York." With that, she sprang from her bed, took the portrait, and walked into the sea. Several days later, the portrait washed ashore off the Outer Banks of North Carolina, and the physician took it home to Elizabeth City. His descendants eventually sold it to a member of the Burr family.

Hundreds of people claim they have seen Theodosia's ghost wandering the beach at Cape Hatteras toward Nags Head between Christmas and New Year's Day, a childlike woman in old-fashioned clothes. At the end of 2001, Paige Rowland & Michael Dietz, actors on such shows as *Beverly Hills 90210*, sought investors for a movie entitled *Theodosia* starring Rowland in the title role and Dietz as Meriwether Lewis.

Based on Anya Seton's 1941 historical novel *My Theodosia*, the movie, if produced as proposed, will bring Theodosia Burr Alston and Meriwether Lewis together once more. In Seton's novel and the proposed motion picture, Theodosia returns Meriwether's obsession.

[‡]Donald Jackson, ed. *Letters of the Lewis and Clark Expedition, With Related Documents*, Second Edition, 2 Volumes (Urbana: University of Illinois Press, 1978). Dillon refers to the first edition, published in 1962. The second edition expands the "bio-bibliography" to twenty pages.

Dillon mentions Lewis's dog (he calls him "Scammon") five times in his biography of Meriwether Lewis:

1. The reference to the Shawnee who offers to buy the dog for three beaverskins and Lewis's note that he paid $20.00 for the dog.

2. A conclusion that "At the start of winter [at Camp Dubois on the Wood River], he [Lewis] was sure of only one member of the expedition besides Clark and himself—his big Newfoundland dog, Scammon."

3. Seaman retrieving geese as the Expedition traveled up the Missouri after leaving the Mandan/Hidatsa villages in 1805: "Scammon delighted his master by bounding into the river to retrieve geese shot by the soldiers, and Lewis, hardly believing his eyes, saw nests of wild geese in tall trees."

4. Seaman barking at grizzlies during the portage around the Great Falls in June 1805: "My dog seems to be in a constant state of alarm with these bears and keeps barking all night."

5. The theft of Seaman on April 11, 1805: "The debilitated condition of the whites gave the Chinooks courage. They threw stone at two soldiers and pushed Shields off the trail. But the last straw for Lewis was when they tried to steal Scammon. A friendly Indian told him that the Newfoundland had been decoyed away. He sent three men in hot pursuit, with orders to fire on the rustlers if they offered the least resistance. The Indians abandoned Lewis's dog and fled. The Virginian reported his anger: 'We ordered the sentinel to keep them out of camp and informed them, by signs, that if they made any further attempts to steal our property, or insulted our men, we should put them to death.' He added, "Our men seem perfectly well disposed to kill a few of them."

Dillon's biography was out-of-print for several decades before being reissued by Western Tanager Press in 1988.

The reference to "Scammon" at the winter quarters on the Wood River appears in the opening paragraph of Chapter VII, "The Advance Base," in which Dillon characterizes Lewis as "The Beau Brummel officer and gentleman who had earned the sobriquet of 'the sublime dandy' transformed himself into a fair likeness of Mad Anthony Wayne."

If Wilson's biography is a "farrago of errors," Dillon's is fraught with tantalizing tidbits that cry for a footnote, like Lewis's reputation as a "sublime dandy."

Dillon's last reference is particularly interesting because of his use of Wilson's favorite sobriquet for Lewis — "the Virginian." Dillon dismisses Wilson in his preface, but he obviously read him.

Seaman graduates to a dozen references in Ambrose's *Undaunted Courage*, where he is listed as "Seaman" in the index. Ambrose has Lewis buying Seaman in Pittsburgh while waiting for the completion of the keelboat. He records Seaman catching squirrels on the Ohio and the Shawnee offer to buy Seaman on November 16, 1803. ("Seaman was always with Lewis," writes Ambrose.) Seaman is noted as a member of the permanent party assembled for departure in the spring of 1804 and as Lewis's sole companion on walks ashore as the Corps makes its way up the Missouri. On April 25, 1805, Seaman returns after being out all night "to Lewis's delight." Buffalo bulls "kept Seaman up all night, barking at them" in June 1805. Ambrose quotes Lewis's report of Seaman "binting and scratching himself as if in a rack of pain" because of the needle grass on July 26, 1805 and the Shoshone being impressed with "the segacity of my dog," as recorded by Lewis on August 17, 1805.

Ambrose includes the theft of Seaman on April 11, 1806:

In the evening, three Indians stole Lewis's dog, Seaman, which sent him into a rage. He called three men and snapped out orders to follow and find those thieves and "if they made the least resistance or difficulty in surrendering the dog to fire on them." The soldiers set out; when the thieves realized they were being pursued, they let Seaman go and fled. Lewis may have been ready to kill to get Seaman back, but the Indians weren't ready to die for the dog.

Ambrose notes Lewis's cryptic "My dog much worried" entry on July 7, 1806 — "apparently referring to the wounded moose [shot by Reubin Field]."

Finally, Ambrose, in his conjectures about Lewis's thoughts as he sat on Mrs. Grinder's porch the evening before he committed suicide, "Did one of Mrs. Grinder's dogs chase a squirrel

As Clay Jenkinson so convincingly documents in his chapter "Deadly Sins: Wrath" in his humanities essays on the character of Lewis, Meriwether had a fierce temper. Although he was able to keep his anger under control during most of the journey to the Pacific, his temper definitely shortened after the miserable winter at Fort Clatsop.

James Ronda suggests that Lewis changed at Fort Clatsop, when he rationalized the Corps' theft of a canoe and characterized natives as *treacherous* — and "moved from common-sense vigilance of the sort required of every explorer to a dangerous flirtation with paranoia."

Why did the theft of Seaman so enrage Lewis that he was ready to kill? Was it just another incident that finally sent him over the edge, or was it indeed because he so loved his faithful Newfoundland that he would kill to get him back?

and remind him of Seaman? Could it be that he thought of that moment of triumph when his canoes put in at St. Louis in September 1806?"

Ambrose implies with his question that Seaman was not there at the end, the night before Meriwether Lewis died. He offers no conjecture about Seaman's fate.

The last reference to Seaman in the journals is on July 15, 1806, when Lewis writes about mosquitoes: "my dog even howls with the torture he experiences from them, they are almost insupportable, they are so numerous that we frequently get them in our thrats as we breath.—"

Unsure that Seaman ever made it back to St. Louis, many historians left him there with the mosquitoes in the American West. The evidence that he did indeed return, that Seaman, in fact, was there with Lewis at the end did not surface until Jim Holmberg of the Filson Historical Society tracked down the story of Seaman's collar and the legend that Lewis's faithful partner died of grief on his friend's grave.[†]

Before Holmberg published his remarkable discovery early in 2000, only one historian — other than the careless Wilson — discussed the eventual fate of Lewis's dog in any detail. Ernest S. Osgood in his "Our Dog Scannon — Partner in Discovery"[††] detailed most of the references in the journals to Seaman. In his delightful and thorough essay, Osgood invoked Homer and Odysseus's return after twenty years to his faithful dog, Argus, who "lay neglected upon a pile of dung." When the dog sees Odysseus,

> . . . he wagged his tail and dropped both ears, but toward his master he had not strength to move. Odysseus turned aside and wiped away a tear . . . But upon Argos fell the darksome doom of death, but he had beheld Odysseus after twenty years.

[†]James J. Holmberg, "Seaman's Fate?" 26 *We Proceeded On* (February 2000), pages 7-9. See more about Holmberg's discovery on pages 59-61, 63.

[††]Ernest Staples Osgood, "Our Dog Scannon — Partner in Discovery," first published in *Montana, The Magazine of History* 26 (July 1976), pp. 8-17, reprinted in *We Proceeded On*, WPO, Supplementary Publication No. 2 (1977,1978, 1981) and in *We Proceeded On*, WPO Publication No. 10 (September 1990).

In his introductory overview of the history of Newfoundland dogs, Osgood included Robert Burns's description of the breed in his "Twa Dogs":

Table-size bronze Meriwether Lewis and 'Our Dog' "Scannon" below was sculpted and cast in a limited edition of 150 by Montanan Robert "Bob" Scriver in 1976.

His hair, his size, his mouth, his lugs (ears)
Showed he was nane o' Scotland's dogs,
But whalpit some place far abroad
Where sailors gang to fish for cod.

Osgood concluded that Seaman could not have been with Lewis on the Marias and there when the small party fled on horseback after the encounter with the Blackfeet. For one thing, he would have given alarm before the Piegan warriors crept into the camp. Moreover, he would not have been able to keep up with the men on horses who covered over a hundred miles after the early morning fight on July 27 to 2:00 A.M. on July 28, 1806. Osgood suggested that Seaman did not go along with the Lewis party of four men on horseback with two packhorses on July 17th to explore the Marias, that he stayed with the main party and was there to greet Lewis when he rode in on July 28th. It was not conceivable to Osgood that Seaman either died or was abandoned: "Not to

"Seaman was always with Lewis," says Stephen E. Ambrose in his narrative of Lewis's trip down the Mississippi in 1803. But was he with Lewis on the trip up the Marias, July 17-28, 1806?

Could a Newfoundland keep up with men mounted on fresh horses as Wilson suggests? "The adventurers pushed on as rapidly as their horses could carry them, Brewster running close beside his master. All day they rode, and when a supper was finished and the dog fed, they pushed on through moonlight. At daybreak the adventurers took a few hours of rest, then remounted and continued the journey."

Seaman, a Newfoundland of incredible endurance, might well have kept up with the horses carrying riders, who traveled at eight miles an hour, by Ambrose's estimation. Moreover, the group broke for dinner after killing a buffalo cow and "again set out by moon light and traveled leasurely," in Lewis's words.

More problematic is the question, "If Seaman was there, why didn't he bark an alarm when the Piegans crept into the camp?"

mention him might suggest a conspiracy of silence. . . . Therefore the evidence, such as it is, points to the conclusion that he was with the party when it arrived at St. Louis."

In his footnote to Lewis's entry for September 11, 1803 in his edition of *The Journals of the Lewis and Clark Expedition*, Gary E. Moulton writes,

> The first mention of Seaman, or Scannon, whose name appears infrequently in the journals. Lewis may have purchased him before reaching Pittsburgh and he served as a hunter, watchdog, and companion. Though not mentioned after July 1806, it has been supposed that he was still with the party on its return in September 1806. A stream in Montana was apparently named for him, leading Don Jackson to conjecture the latest spelling of his name.[†]

In their 1959 book for children (*Scannon: Dog with Lewis and Clark*), Adrien Stoutenburg and Laura Nelson Baker present a highly-readable and mostly accurate account of the Expedition and of many of the episodes which feature Seaman in the journals of members of the Corps of Discovery. They do place "Scannon" with Lewis, the Field Brothers, and Drouillard at the encounter with the Blackfeet, and the dog is as surprised as everyone else when Lewis awakens:

> Joseph Fields [most scholars now spell the name *Field*] was on guard duty

---

†Gary E. Moulton, ed. *The Journals of the Lewis and Clark Expedition*, Volume 2, August 30, 1803-August 24, 1804 (Lincoln and London: University of Nebraska Press, 1986), p. 80.

If Seaman had problems keeping up with the party on horseback fleeing the scene of the encounter with the Blackfeet, he certainly would have been able to track them and catch up the next day in the fashion related in the Stoutenburg/Baker book.

Osgood's most compelling reason for his conclusion that Seaman was not with Lewis on the Marias is his failure to bark alarm. A close reading of Lewis's journal allows for another explanation. The four explorers were camped with the Blackfeet, and Lewis was comfortable enough to write two thousand words in his journal about the day. As Ambrose notes, "He covered it from start to finish, with frequent interruptions to the narrative. . . . Mainly, though, he described what had happened in an after-action report. At half past eleven, he roused Reubin Field. He ordered Field to watch the movements of the Indians and if one of them left camp to awake the party, lest the Indians attempt to steal the detachment's horses. Then he lay down and immediately fell into a profound sleep."

Seaman had slept near Lewis on hundreds of nights, and on many of those nights there were Indians nearby. Seaman took his cue from Lewis, who slept soundly even though Indians were nearby. If Seaman was awake, he did not consider the Indians as a threat because they did not try to touch Lewis or any other member of the party.

at dawn. Lewis woke at his cry of alarm to see Drouilliard wrestling with an Indian who was trying to steal his gun. Through the tent opening he saw both of the Fields brothers racing after another Indian who had taken their rifles. Lewis leaped up, reaching for his own similar weapon. It was gone. He had his hand on his pistol in its holster when he saw one of the Blackfoot hurrying off with his rifle. He rushed after him. The Indian turned, saw the pistol aimed at his heart, and dropped Lewis' rifle.

Ahead, Reuben [his name is usually spelled *Reubin*] Fields was drawing a dripping knife from the chest of the Indian who had been trying to get away with the two rifles. Drouilliard had won his contest with the other native and ran forward to point his gun at the Indian who had stolen Lewis' gun.

"Let him be," Lewis ordered, and turned to give chase to Indians who were trying to drive off his and his men's horses. One of the Indians was lashing Lewis' own horse before him. At Lewis' shout to give the horse back, the Indian turned, his gun pointed at Lewis. But Lewis was faster. His rifle blasted. The Indian fell to his knees and crawled behind a rock, bringing his own gun up into firing position. A bullet whistled past Lewis' bare head.

Lewis reached for his shot pouch to reload his rifle but the pouch was back in the tent. He hurried back to the camp, where he was joined by the others.

"They take five of our horses," Drouilliard panted. "But they leave in mistake twelve of their own!" "Round up as many as you can!" Lewis ordered. "We'll need them. The Blackfoot will be back as soon as they can reorganize their forces."

The Fields brothers, taking Scannon with them, set out after the Indian horses. In his excitement, Scannon raced in wild circles around the frightened ponies, barking until he was hoarse.

The men recovered four of their own horses and several of those belonging to the Indians. As soon as they could get their saddles and supplies in order, they set out to put as much distance between them and the Blackfoot as possible. Equally important, they must warn the party left on the Missouri, for the Blackfoot might strike there first.

"You'll have to keep up as best you can, Scannon," Lewis said as he swung up on a horse.

Scannon took after the galloping mounts, racing as fast as his legs could carry him. But it was impossible to keep up. Little by little the distance between him and the riders widened. No matter how hard he tried, his legs were no match for those of the swift ponies. Gamely he kept on going, his tongue lolling, his ribs working for breath, but soon the riders were merely moving dots far ahead. Finally, there was not even that. He was alone, loping on and on over the level trail, the only visibly moving thing, except for buffalo, in miles and miles of prairie.
. . . .

Seaman keeps traveling. Lewis and the men reach the Missouri and meet Sergeant Ordway and the other nine men who had come to join Lewis. Ordway asks, "Where's Scannon?"

Lewis looked back along the trail. "He'll be along." He said it confidently but the men heard the concern in his voice.

Thunder rattled the sky and lightning flashes brightened the whole landscape with an eerie radiance. Lewis lay huddled under a blanket, water soaking into his clothes, for there had been no time or materials for building a shelter. Another rattling peal of thunder shook the sky—and right behind it came a bark.

Lewis sat up, his heart beating swiftly. He peered through the rain. Lightning sent a shuddering bolt of yellow across the camp site. In its brief brilliance he saw a big black dog—or the ghost of a dog—limping toward him.

"Scannon!" Lewis shouted and went sloshing toward him. "Scannon," he said again, kneeling down and holding the dog's wet head against his chest. He looked up to see Ordway grinning down at him. "I said he'd be along," Lewis reminded the sergeant with an answering grin.

All things considered, *Scannon, Dog with Lewis and Clark* tells Seaman's tale with remarkable fidelity to the journals. It reflects the best scholarship available at the time. Decades before Ernest Osgood concluded that Seaman must have returned, the authors bring Lewis's dog back to St. Louis, ready to go along to Washington to report to President Jefferson.

Stoutenburg and Baker underestimate the stamina and endurance of Newfoundlands, but not their loyalty and persistence. Moreover, the seasoned explorers and their judicious leader did not "gallop" their mounts, because they knew they had a long way to go.

We know that Lewis was ready to kill for his dog in April 1806. His relationship with Seaman was such that he would never have said, "You'll have to keep up as best you can."

As the nation approached the bicentennial of the Lewis and Clark Expedition in the late 1990s, more attention was paid to Lewis's faithful companion. In 1999, former wolf biologist Roland Smith released *The Captain's Dog: My Journey with the Lewis and Clark Tribe*.[†] Smith's delightful tale begins with John Colter and George Drouillard finding Seaman with Twisted Hair's Nez Percé camp years after the Expedition. Seaman is with the old woman Watkuweis and her people. The young guide who helped the Corps, Mountain Dog, had brought Seaman and Lewis's journal to camp after the Corps departed in 1806. Around a campfire, the returning explorers and Nez Percé read the story of the Expedition, and Seaman tells his tale in first-person. At the end, Seaman explains how he came to be with the Nez Percé (the ending deserves to be read in the original, not revealed here).

Cover of The Captain's Dog *by Roland Smith, who observes in his "Author's Note" at the end of the book, "Dogs spend more time watching us than we do watching them. As a result, I believe they know a great deal more about us than we know about them. A dog sees, hears, and smells things we cannot dream of perceiving. Who better to tell this story than the Captain's extraordinary dog?*

Smith places Seaman with Lewis on the Marias as well, but in *The Captain's Dog*, Seaman doesn't catch up with the men on horseback. He is not seen until Drouillard and Colter find him years later with the Nez Percé after Lewis shouts back to his dog, "Let's go, Sea." Seaman lives, but he never leaves the American West.

Seaman also lives to return to the Mandan/Hidatsa villages in Gail Langer Karwoski's *Seaman: The Dog Who Explored the West with Lewis and Clark*,[‡] but he does not return to St. Louis. Seaman stays with John Colter, a man born to live in the West. As Clay Jenkinson says at the conclusion of his books of essays on Meriwether Lewis, "Some men don't belong in the wilderness: Charbonneau. Some don't belong in civilization: John Colter.

[†]Roland Smith, *The Captain's Dog: My Journey with the Lewis and Clark Tribe* (New York: Gulliver Books, Harcourt, Inc., 1999).

[‡]Gail Langer Karwoski, *Seaman: The Dog Who Explored the West with Lewis and Clark,* illustrated by James Watling (Atlanta: Peachtree Publishers, Ltd., 1999).

And a few, having spent time in both, find they no longer have a home in either world [Lewis]."

In her finely-crafted, carefully-researched story of Seaman, wonderfully illustrated by James Watling, Karwoski chooses to return Seaman to the West instead of sending him back with Lewis, who, in Jenkinson's astute phrase, returned from his experience a man with a home neither in the wilderness or in "civilization." She also leaves Seaman with the group of explorers on the Missouri while Lewis and three men go up the Marias:

Cover of Seaman: The Dog Who Explored the West with Lewis and Clark.

> Before he left camp, he called Seaman. "I'm going to leave you here at the river, fellow."

> Seaman cocked his head as Lewis talked.

> Lewis grinned at the alert expression on the dog's face. He knelt and stroked Seaman's head. "Seaman, I need you to guard our camp again," he said, rubbing the thick fur on Seaman's chest.

> As soon as Lewis stood up, Seaman scrambled to his feet. "Stay, Seaman," Lewis said. He mounted his horse.

> Seaman sat, watching Lewis's face eagerly.

> Lewis told the men to keep the dog in camp so he wouldn't follow the horse. Then he and the scouts rode away

Karwoski, a gifted storyteller, obviously studied the journals of the members of the Corps of Discovery and did extensive research, which she summarizes at the end of her book. In her "Author's Note" to later editions, she addresses the question, "What happened to Seaman, Captain Lewis's beloved New-foundland dog?" Her answer led me to a search for Timothy Alden's 1814 *A Collection of American Epitaphs and Inscriptions with Occasional Notes*, the source of the intriguing note that has the faithful Seaman dying of grief in 1809 on Meriwether Lewis's grave.

Karwoski found the information after she wrote her book, and she included the reference in a revision because she wanted to be as accurate as possible. The sleuth who discovered Alden's note, James J. Holmberg, tracked back a reference to Seaman's eventual fate in the Louisville (Kentucky) *Public Advertiser*, May 5, 1835.[†]

I finally found Alden's words in a 1977 facsimile edition by Arno Press.[††]

Below, Title Page from Volume V of Timothy Alden's 1814 Publication.

A

COLLECTION

OF

AMERICAN EPITAPHS

AND

INSCRIPTIONS

WITH

OCCASIONAL NOTES.

BY REV. TIMOTHY ALDEN, A. M.

HONORARY MEMBER OF THE MASSACHUSETTS AND OF THE NEW-YORK HISTORICAL SOCIETIES, MEMBER OF THE AMERICAN ANTIQUA- RIAN SOCIETY, ETC.

PENTADE I. VOL. V.

NEW-YORK :

1814

ALEXANDRIA, D. COL.

916. The greatest traveller of my species. My name is Seaman, the dog of captain Meriwether Lewis, whom I accompanied to the Pacifick ocean through the interior of the continent of North America.

Note.— The foregoing was copied from the collar, in the Alexandria Museum, which the late gov. Lewis's dog wore after his return from the western coast of America. The fidelity and attachment of this animal were remarkable. After the melancholy exit of gov. Lewis, his dog would not depart for a moment from his lifeless remains; and when they were deposited in the earth no gentle means could draw him from the spot of interment. He refused to take every kind of food, which was offered him, and actually pined away and died with grief upon his master's grave!

[†]James J. Holmberg, "Seaman's Fate?" 26 *We Proceeded On* (February 2000), pages 7-9. I did not know of Holmberg's remarkable find until after I had waded through most of Alden's 1,500 pages and found the reference for myself. Holmberg found the key, the "article" number.

[††]Rev. Timothy Alden, A.M., *A Collection of American Epitaphs and Inscriptions with Occasional Notes*, Two Volumes (Originally published privately in New York in five volumes, 1814, reprinted in two volumes from copies in the Pennsylvania State Library by Arno Press, a New York Times Company, 1977, as a volume in the Arno Press collection, *The Literature of Dying and Death*). The note about Seaman appears on page 98 of Alden's original Volume V.

Finding the reference before I read Holmberg was no easy task: although the names of the dead people eulogized in Alden's work were indexed, Seaman the dog was not. As I turned nearly 1,500 pages, I discovered many interesting notes, including the source of Longfellow's "The Courtship of Miles Standish" and the love triangle of Rev. Timothy Alden's ancestor, "Speak-for-yourself-John" Alden, Priscilla Mullins, and Captain Miles Standish.[†]

Finally, two-thirds of the way through the second book of the Arno Press reprint, I found Alden's article 916 on Seaman.

98

ALEXANDRIA, D. COL.

916. **The greatest traveller of my species. My name is** Seaman, **the dog of captain Meriwether Lewis, whom I accompanied to the Pacifick ocean through the interior of the continent of North America.**

Note.—The foregoing was copied from the collar, in the Alexandria Museum, which the late gov. Lewis's dog wore after his return from the western coast of America. The fidelity and attachment of this animal were remarkable. After the melancholy exit of gov. Lewis, his dog would not depart for a moment from his lifeless remains; and when they were deposited in the earth no gentle means could draw him from the spot of interment. He refused to take every kind of food, which was offered him, and actually pined away and died with grief upon his master's grave!

[†]The source of Priscilla Mullin's immortal "Speak for yourself, John" is found on pages 264-266 of the original Volume III, Article 620. After his wife Rose dies, Miles Standish sends John Alden to ask for the hand of Priscilla Mullin. "John Alden, the messenger, went and faithfully communicated the wishes of the captain." Priscilla's father consents, with the caveat, that ". . . they young lady must also be consented. The damsel was then called into the room, and John Alden, who is said to have been a man of most excellent form with a fair and ruddy complexion, arose, and, in a very courteous and prepossessing manner, delivered his errand. Miss Mullins listened with resentful attention, and at last, after a considerable pause, fixing her eyes upon him, with an open and pleasant countenance, said, *prithee, John, why do you not speak for yourself?* He blushed, and bowed, and took his leave, but with a look which indicated more than his diffidence would permit him otherwise to express. However, he soon renewed his visit, and it was not long before their nupials were celebrated in ample form. From them are descended all of the name, Alden, in the United States. What report he made to his constituent, after the first interview, tradition does not unfold; but it is said, how true the writer knows not, that the captain never forgave him to the day of his death."

In pages before the note on Seaman's collar, I discovered that the museum where Seaman's collar was on exhibit (probably until the building was destroyed by fire on May 19, 1871) was established under the jurisdiction of "Alexandria Washington Lodge Num. 22" (Masonic Lodge in Alexandria, Virginia). Timothy Mounteford conceived the idea for a museum "on St. John's day, in 1812," and

> A constitution was formed embracing all the ideas of the projector [Mounteford], who was elected by the suffrages of the masonick body the Manager of the Museum."

In addition to Seaman's collar, "among the many thousands articles," were

> . . . the mantle in which Washington received baptism; his grand masonick robes; his pistols studded with brilliants, given by Louis XVI, to the general, through the hands of marquis De La Fayette; a model of the Bastile, made of stone taken from the ruins of that once prison of misery and despair, presented to the general by the national assembly of France.

"These articles," says Alden,

> . . . were given to the Museum by connexions of general Washington, messrs. Lewis, Custis, and Robinson. Other donations of great value have been made by president Madison and other distinguished characters.

Five short years after Lewis's death, a book published in New York correctly names his faithful Newfoundland and notes what happened to him. In fact, Alden gives space in his book equal to the rather cryptic epitaph for Meriwether Lewis (Article 1036, pages 212-213 of the original Volume V):

> 1036. *Note*—His excellency, MERIWETHER LEWIS, the late governour of Louisiana, was born, on the 18 of August, 1774, near Charlottesville in the county of Albermarle and state of Virginia. His father, William Lewis, was the youngest of five sons of colonel Robert Lewis, a brother of colonel Fielding Lewis, of whom a concise notice appears in the 891 article of this Collection.

> In September, 1809, he left the Chickasaw Bluffs, in order to go to Washington. Having passed the Tennessee one day's journey, he put up at the house of a person, by the name of

Grinder. He showed signs of derangement, as he had done at times before, and there, unhappily, put an end to his life.

A very valuable biographical sketch of gov. Lewis, written by mr. Jefferson, is prefixed to the History of the Expedition under the command of Lewis and Clark. This work, published by mr. Paul Allen, in 2 vol. 8vo. with maps, contains a minute and interesting account of the discoveries of these enterprising adventurers in their course to the head of the Missouri, across the Rocky Mountains, and down the Columbia to the Pacifick Ocean.

Jim Holmberg offers the possibility that the donor of the collar to the museum "may have been none other than William Clark."† An official of the Alexandria-Washington Lodge #22 wrote to William Clark in 1812 thanking him for the "truly valuable Present made by you to our Museum. . . ." The very existence of the note in an 1814 publication substantiates Donald Jackson's discovery by way of a close examination of the journals that Lewis's dog was named Seaman, not "Scannon" or "Scammon."

After more hours than I care to count rummaging in Alden's curious volumes, I conclude that he included the note about Seaman's death on Captain Lewis's grave on the basis of something more than an unsubstantiated story — most probably, a label next to the collar in the museum. In the hundreds of pages in five volumes, the Reverend Timothy Alden relies on primary sources, including inscriptions on tombstones and eulogies printed in newspapers or in other publications. For example, his note on Meriwether Lewis, including the sentence, "He showed signs of derangement, as he had done at times before, and there, unhappily, put an end to his life," is based upon Jefferson's biographical sketch printed in the first publication of the journals of Lewis and Clark in 1814. When he speculates, he says so, as he does when he summarizes Miles Standish's reaction to John Alden pursuing Priscilla Mullin for himself: ". . . but it is said, how true the writer knows not, that the captain never forgave him to the day of his death."

---

†James J. Holmberg, "Seaman's Fate?" 26 *We Proceeded On* (February 2000), pages 7-9. Holmberg, the curator of special collections of the Filson Historical Society, in Louisville, Kentucky, indicates in his article that Seaman's collar was probably in the museum at least two years before Alden's publication in 1814.

While it is conceivable that the collar existed as a memorial to a famous dog, not as a piece designed for and worn by Seaman himself, nothing in Alden's presentation indicates anything other than his statement that the inscription ". . . *was copied from the collar, in the Alexandria Museum, which the late gov. Lewis's dog wore after his return* from the western coast of America" [emphasis added]. In short, there is no evidence that Alden is not reporting common knowledge when he records the way in which Seaman died in grief after Meriwether Lewis committed suicide in October 1809. Such is the nature of Newfoundlands, dogs like Lord Byron's Boatswain,

. . . in life the firmest friend,
The first to welcome, foremost to defend;
Whose honest heart is still his master's own,
Who labours, fights, lives, breathes, for him alone. . . .

Byron is buried at Hucknall Torkard Parish Church, Saint Mary Magdalen, in Nottingham, England. His remains were sent from Greece, where he died in April 1824. Authorities would not permit his burial in Westminster Abbey, and there is neither bust nor statue of Lord Byron in Poets' Corner. Lines from his "Childe Harold's Pilgrimage" are inscribed on a marker:

. . . .
But there is that within me which shall tire
Torture and Time, and breathe when I expire
. . . .

NO POEM IS INSCRIBED on Meriwether Lewis's monument. Instead, words from one of America's greatest prose masters, Thomas Jefferson†, whose words, as John Adams said, "were

---

†Jefferson's quote comes from an 1813 letter to Paul Allen, editor of the journals published in 1814. In one of the grand, extended sentences of American prose, Jefferson wrote, "Of courage undaunted, possessing a firmness & perseverance of purpose which nothing but impossibilites could divert from it's direction, careful as a father of those committed to his charge, yet steady in the maintenance of order & discipline, intimate with the Indian character, customs & principles, habituated to the hunting life, guarded by exact observation of the vegetables & animals of his own country, against losing time in the description of objects already possessed, honest, disinterested, liberal, of sound understanding and a fidelity to truth so scrupulous that whatever he should report would be as certain as if seen by ourselves, with all these qualifications as if selected and implanted by nature in one body, for this express purpose, I could have no hesitation in confiding the enterprize to him." — Donald Jackson, ed. *Letters of the Lewis and Clark Expedition, With Related Documents*, Second Edition, 2 Volumes (Urbana: University of Illinois Press, 1978), pages 589-590.

remarkable for . . . peculiar felicity of expression," grace the east face of the broken shaft over his grave:

> His courage was undaunted; His Firmness and Perseverance Yielded to Nothing but Impossibilities; a Rigid Disciplinarian, Yet Tender as a Father of Those Committed to his Charge; Honest, Disinterested, Liberal, with a Sound Understanding and Scrupulous Fidelity to Truth.

AND NO POEM is inscribed in stone immortalizing Seaman, that "greatest Traveller" of his species, "the dog of captain Meriwether Lewis, whom I accompanied to the Pacifick ocean through the interior of the continent of North America."

MAY MY POOR VERSES INSPIRE POETS with far more "felicitous expression" than I can command to write a tribute to Captain Meriwether Lewis's most loyal friend, and may those words be carved in stone somewhere near the grave on which Seaman died with grief over the departure of his troubled friend.

Everett C. Albers
Bismarck, North Dakota
Christmas Day, 2001

I am the noble Newfoundland,
My voice is loud and deep;
I keep a watch all through the night
While other people sleep.

Anonymous Late-Nineteenth Century Children's Song

About the Author . . .

Everett C. Albers has served as the executive director of The
North Dakota Humanities Council, the state partner of the
National Endowment for the Humanities, since it began in
1973. Albers is one of the founders of the modern Chautauqua
movement which features first-person characterizations of
historical writers and thinkers presented in tents during
summer tours of the Great Plains. He holds an M.A. in English
from Colorado State University and has taught humanities and
English. A North Dakota native who grew up with a loyal dog
named Curly on a family homestead in Oliver County, Albers
lives with his wife Leslie in Bismarck. They are the parents of
Albert and Gretchen. Albers operates Otto Design, a desktop
publishing concern, as an avocation. He has co-edited several
books, including a six-part series, *The Way It Was: North
Dakota's Frontier Experience*, collections of stories of the
earliest North Dakota pioneers selected from nearly 5,000
interviews gathered in a Works Progress Administration
project in the 1930s; *The Legacy of North Dakota Country
Schools, Behold Our New Century: Early 20th Century Visions
of America,* and *100 Or So North Dakota Centenarians at the
End of the 20th Century*. Albers has written several children's
coloring books featuring Seaman and has designed and written
text for a five-part series of collector's cards featuring the
members of the Corps of Discovery and the American Indians
they encountered.